El

Rancho

In

South

Texas

EL

RANCHO

IN

SOUTH

TEXAS

Continuity

and Change

from 1750

Joe S. Graham

John E. Conner Museum
Texas A & M University—Kingsville

University of North Texas Press

Printed in the United States of America

First Edition 1994

10 9 8 7 6 5 4 3 2 1

Requests for permission to reproduce material from this
work should be sent to:

Permissions

University of North Texas Press

Post Office Box 13856

Denton, Texas 76203-6856

The paper used in this book meets the minimum
requirements of the American National Standard for
Permanence of Paper for Printed Library materials,
Z39.48.1984. Binding materials have been chosen for
durability.

Cover illustration by Charles Shaw

Library of Congress Cataloging-in-Publication Data

Graham, Joe Stanley.

   El Rancho in South Texas: continuity and change from
1750/Joe S. Graham.

   p. cm.

   Includes bibliographical references and index.

   ISBN 0-929398-58-0

   1. Ranch life—Texas—History—Exhibitions.
2. Ranches—Texas—History—Exhibitions.   3. Texas—
History, Local—Exhibitions.   4. Texas—Social life and
customs—Exhibitions.   I. Title.

F386.G65 1993

976.4—dc20   93-32211

                                              CIP

Acknowledgments

for Exhibit

and Catalog

Major Funding Sources

The National Endowment for the Humanities

The Meadows Foundation

The John E. Conner Museum, Texas A&M
  University—Kingsville

Exhibit Design

David Garrison, The University of Texas Institute
  of Texan Cultures

Consultants

Dr. David Montejano
Dept. of History
Univ. of Texas at Austin

Dr. Eugene George, Jr.
Dept. of Architecture
Univ. of Texas at Austin

Dr. José Roberto Juárez
Dept. of History
St. Edwards University

Richard Ahlborn
Division of Community Life
Natural Museum of American History
The Smithsonian Institution

Lonn Taylor
Natural Museum of American History
The Smithsonian Institution

Dr. Janet R. Fireman
Natural History Museum of Los Angeles County

William Charles Bennett, Jr.
Palace of the Governors
Museum of New Mexico

Dr. Arnoldo De Léon
Dept. of History
Angelo State University

David Haynes
University of Texas Institute of Texan Cultures

Dr. George O. Coalson
Dept. of History
Texas A&M University—Kingsville

Dr. Andres Tijerina
Dept. of History
Texas A&M University—Kingsville

Contents

Preface

This book, *El Rancho in South Texas: Continuity and Change from 1750,* is based on the first major exhibit to examine the private cattle ranch in South Texas, held in 1994 in the John E. Conner Museum in Kingsville, Texas. Ranching has been the basis for civilization and culture in the region for well over a century and a half. It was a way of life for the majority of people living there, and its importance continues today, not only with famous spreads like the King Ranch but with the hundreds of smaller ones on which many communities in South Texas continue to rely for their identity and survival. Many towns, large and small, actually began as ranch headquarters.

While many early ranches relied upon sheep as their main source of income well into the twentieth century, the exhibit and this book focus on the cattle ranch, which has become dominant in the region. Ironically, although such scholars as Walter Prescott Webb have recognized South Texas as the cradle of the cattle industry, there has been little scholarly effort focused on the ranch and its culture in this region, other than histories of specific ranches. The exhibit and the book are designed to examine the ranching culture and to place it in its historical context.

By 1750, when the private cattle ranch arrived in South Texas, it had been evolving in Spain and Mexico for over seven centuries. The first Spanish settlers arrived with a culture which permitted them to successfully settle this arid land and make it productive. They brought with them their architecture, which had its roots in Spain and among Indian populations in Mexico; the social structure of the *hacienda,* with its

two distinct social classes; the knowledge of how to tend cattle most effectively and how to find and produce enough water to raise large herds of cattle in this arid region. It also included the gender-defined work roles, the clothing and equipment, and the foodways and medical knowledge of the *vaqueros* and other early settlers.

Many of the published studies of the South Texas region are incomplete, given the fact that much of the information about the first century of its history remains in archives in Mexico. Hopefully, South Texas ranching will one day have a study like Jack Jackson's *Los Mesteños* focused on it.

The best records currently available for South Texas are those associated with its Anglo ranches and ranching history. These first Anglos adopted the Spanish/Mexican institution, including the knowledge, equipment, and skills for raising and managing large herds of cattle. When they came into the region, they brought their Anglo laws governing land ownership, their business skills and contacts for developing a strong market economy, and new technologies which would eventually transform the ranch into its modern form. They also brought their own architectural styles and social customs, adapting them to the circumstances they found here.

The fact that *el rancho* has survived as a social institution for close to ten centuries indicates its adaptability to changing social, political, and cultural circumstances. While Mexican Americans continue to own much of the land along the Rio Grande, most of the land toward the Nueces River now belongs to Anglos. Nevertheless, as in the past, the vast majority of the *vaqueros* and cowboys working on these ranches are of Mexican ancestry. Many come from families which have worked in the region for generations. The Spanish language continues to be an important means of communication, as most Anglos working on ranches—including the ranch foremen and owners—speak Spanish with their *vaqueros*.

Those of us who have lived for some time in the American Southwest and West have come to appreciate the effect which Mexican Americans and their ancestors have had on our culture. Major contributions to the foodways, music, celebrations, architecture, and place-names found throughout the region are readily recognizable. After all, what would the region be without enchiladas, tacos, and tortillas? Without "*Las Mañanitas*" and "*La Cucaracha*," and, more recently, *mariachi* and *conjunto* music? Without such public and private celebrations as *las posadas* and the *quinceañera*? Without the adobe architecture which so clearly marks life in West Texas, New Mexico, Arizona and other western states?

But this cultural contribution is as great or greater in a number of additional areas, perhaps one of the most significant being the social institution called *el rancho*— the ranch—and its culture. Not only was the ranch the primary social unit used to settle the West and Southwest, but its culture provides the genesis of America's greatest mythic hero, the cowboy. While some have recognized this major contribution to American culture as Spanish and Mexican, others have assumed it to be Anglo American in origin. J. Frank Dobie gives us a clear perspective on the issue, noting that years before the first English colony was established in North America, a single rancher in the Mexican province of Jalisco was "branding 30,000 calves a year," and that in Durango and southern Chihuahua there were individual herds "numbering in the tens of thousands" (1941). As a matter of fact, records show that in 1578, Francisco de Ibarra, who had ranches in the borderlands of Zacatecas and Durango, owned about 130,000 head of cattle, and in the year 1586 branded 33,000 calves. Several ranchers of this era branded over 30,000 calves every year, not counting those which ran wild (Dary 1981). Río de la Loza, one of these ranchers, branded some 42,000 calves a year (Brand 1961).

There is no doubt that Anglos of the old South (particularly the Carolinas) had begun developing systems of livestock raising and management based on the earlier British system, but when they came into contact with ranching in Texas in the early 1800s, they adopted the system of land and cattle management which the Spaniards and later the Mexicans had developed over several centuries. Anglo contributions to the ranching industry, including the introduction of new breeds of cattle and such new technologies as barbed wire, drilling equipment, and windmills, came after the Civil War. Anglos played a major role in transforming ranching from a traditional way of life to a profit-making, market-oriented industry, beginning with the cattle drives to northern markets. Railroads eliminated long cattle drives, but the stockyards and packing plants would continue to the present. Anglos also played the major role in the spread of the private cattle ranch from South Texas into the greater Southwest.

The ranch and its culture provide perhaps the best example of a successful confluence of Spanish and Anglo cultures in any modern social organization. Of the three social institutions introduced by the Spanish—the mission, the *presidio,* and the ranch—only the ranch continues. And long after the political, financial, and social influence of Spain ended in this part of the world, the ranch has remained a viable, productive and significant part of our culture—both economically and culturally—particularly in South Texas.

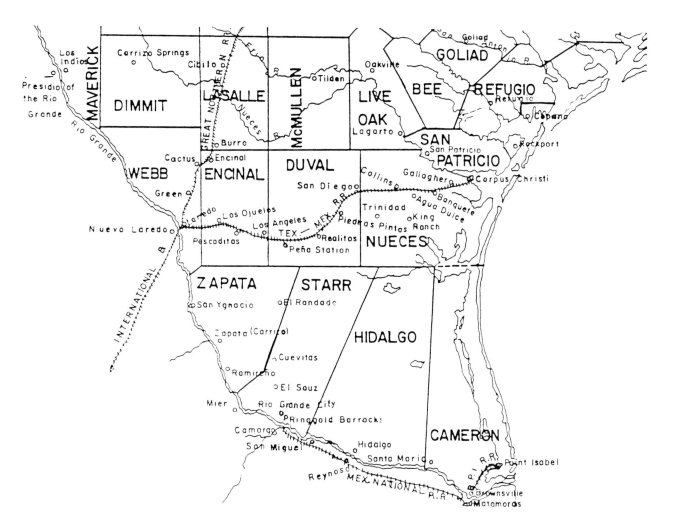

Map of South Texas. Courtesy of Agnes Grimm.

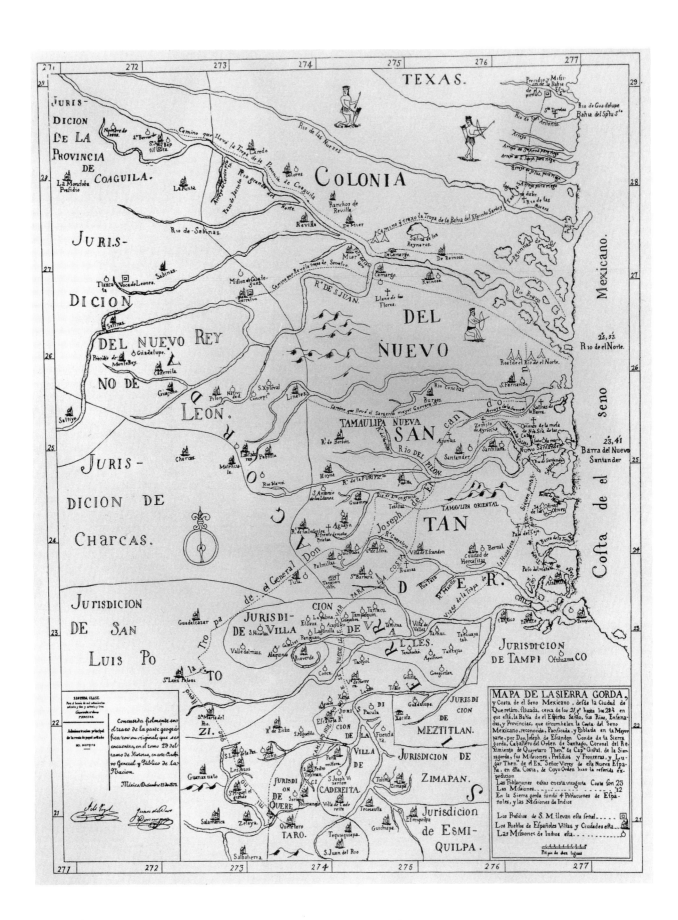

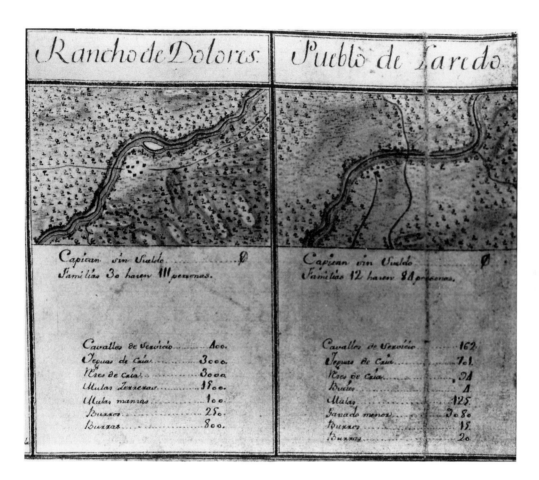

Left: Provencia de Nuevo Santander. Escandón and 3000 colonists and soldiers settled in Nuevo Santander in 1749. By 1755, there were 23 settlements. Original by Tomas Sánchez, 1755, found in Archivo General y Público, Mexico, Historia, vol. 29. Courtesy University of California Press, Berkeley.

Above: A map from the 1757 Cuervo report of two early ranches: Nuestra Señora de los Dolores and San Augustín de Laredo, with livestock inventories. Courtesy British Library.

Facing page, top: Coastal Prairie. Along with the Riparian Forest and the dry brushland, this was the type of environment the earliest Europeans would have encountered. Courtesy John E. Conner Museum.

Facing page, bottom: South Texas Grasslands with Riparian Forest in the distance. This is the type of environment which covered most of South Texas when Escandón first saw it. Courtesy John E. Conner Museum.

Above: Dry brushland is an environment still found in much of South Texas. Courtesy John E. Conner Museum.

Spanish Exploration and Settlement of Texas

Spanish exploration of Texas began in 1519, when Alsonso Àlvarez de Pineda spent six months mapping the coast between Florida and Tampico, Mexico, providing the first accurate map of the Texas Gulf Coast. He did no exploring beyond mapping, and did not travel across land. The first European explorers known to have actually traveled through this part of Texas came with Alvar Núñez Cabeza de Vaca. He and three companions, members of the ill-fated Pánfilo de Narváez expedition which shipwrecked near Galveston Island, were rescued by the Karankawa Indians and spent the following eight years as slaves, as traders, and finally as healers. Cabeza de Vaca's diary, written in 1542, provides the first descriptions of South and West Texas. Because his descriptions were not encouraging, exploration into Texas and other parts of the Southwest ceased for some forty years. During this time, however, the Mexican frontier continued to be pushed northward by ranchers seeking land for their growing herds of cattle and other livestock, by miners and soldiers continuing their search for precious metals, and by missionaries seeking converts for the Church.

As the Spanish soldiers, miners, missionaries, and settlers pushed the Mexican frontier farther north, they brought with them three principal institutions: missions, established as religious centers; *presidios*, established as military outposts; and ranches, established as residences. They settled in four areas of Texas, three of which remain Hispanic population centers even today. These four regions include the El Paso region of West Texas, East Texas in the Nacogdoches area, the San Antonio area (including the Refugio/Victoria area), and South Texas (south of the Nueces River).

Missions in Texas

Missions functioned as agencies for both the state and the church. In the eyes of the latter, their chief function was to spread Christianity to the heathen inhabitants. From the point of view of the Spanish Crown, missionaries were to serve as both explorers and diplomats, so that missions would play a role in extending the Spanish frontiers (Weddle 1992).

While the Franciscans gave religious instruction to the natives, they also taught them about agriculture and industry, including the rudiments of cultivating and harvesting crops and caring for livestock—horses, cattle, sheep, goats, and hogs. In effect, then, these early missions also functioned as ranches, with the Crown furnishing the land and the church furnishing the livestock. In 1768, Fray José de Solís, Inspector of Missions for the College of Zacatecas, reported that the missions at San Antonio owned about 5,487 cattle, over 600 saddle horses and about 1,000 breeding mares, over 100 burros and about 100 mules, and around 17,000 sheep and goats. That same year, Mission Espíritu Santo at Goliad claimed about 5,000 cattle and 200 milk cows, along with about 100 horses, 30 mules, and as many as 7,000 sheep and goats (Lehmann 1969). Because the missions did not maintain control over many of their cattle, large herds of *mesteños*—wild, unbranded cattle—grew in the regions surrounding the missions.

Between 1682 and 1793, as many as forty-one missions were established by the Franciscan missionaries in Texas. Some of these lasted less than a year, while others lasted over a century before being secularized. At any given time, however, there were hardly more than a dozen in operation (Weddle 1992).

Four missions were established in the El Paso region before 1795, and five missions were established in the La Junta (Presidio, Texas) area. In East Texas, a total of nine missions operated at one time or another between 1690 and 1773. The early ones were abandoned shortly after they began, but in 1721 they were re-established along with the Presidio de Nuestra Señora de Pilar de los Adaes near Mission San Miguel, which served as the capital of the Province of Texas for half a century.

Between 1719 and 1830, seven missions operated in the San Antonio area and six others between the present-day town of Goliad and the Gulf Coast. These would play an important role in the development of mission ranching activity until the missions in the San Antonio area were secularized in 1824. The two missions in Goliad—Espíritu Santo and Rosario—were not secularized until 1830 and 1831, respectively.

Presidios in Texas

During this same period of time, the Spanish government established twelve *presidios* to serve and protect the missions and settlements in Texas, eight of which were located within the present boundaries of the state. Of these twelve, three were in the West Texas region, three were in East Texas, and three were in the San Antonio/Goliad region. Another existed briefly (about five years) between the Colorado and Brazos rivers, and still another one near Menard on a branch of the Conchos River lasted about thirteen years. An additional *presidio* was established in 1701 to protect the missions near Eagle Pass, and it lasted until 1821.

Presidios had four main functions: (1) to protect the missions, (2) to campaign against hostile Indians, (3) to accompany supply trains, and (4) to explore new territory (Weddle 1992). Because of this, the *presidios* had no direct connection to the development of ranching, although many of the officers and soldiers associated with them became involved in private ranching in various regions of the state.

The Ranch: A Spanish Institution

Although cattle could be found throughout Europe and much of the rest of the civilized world during the Middle Ages, the development of the ranch as a social institution can be claimed by Spain. Bishko states that "a genuine ranch cattle industry evolved in the Peninsula in the later eleventh and twelfth centuries, under Alfonso VI and Alfonso VII of León-Castile" (1952). Its birthplace, he argues, was "that portion of the sub-humid or arid interior tableland of the Meseta Central lying between the middle course of the Duere River and the massive sierras of Gata, Gredos and Guadarrama; or, more specifically, the *tierras* of Zamora and Salamanca in León, and those of Segovia and Avila in southern Old Castile" (1952). During the later Middle Ages, the Andalusian plains became the one region of the Peninsula (and perhaps all of Europe) where agriculture and the pastoral life were dominated by a "thriving, highly organized cattle-ranching economy" (1952). Many of the Spanish colonists who would settle in the Canary Islands and the Indies came from this region.

One of the primary factors leading to the development of ranching was the type of cattle which developed in the Andalusian plains. Because they were unsuited for dairy or draft purposes, the owners and their workers had to abandon the small cow pastures for the open range, leading to the use of horses for herding and the development of a method for managing cattle in such a system: long-distance grazing, periodic roundups, branding, overland cattle drives—in short, the invention of cattle ranching. The co-existence of herded, branded cattle and wild, ownerless ones was a common feature of peninsular cattle raising long before it crossed the ocean to Española, New Spain, Brazil, and eventually to South Texas.

Before 1500 A.D., when some herds in the Caribbean ran as many as 20,000 head or more, the Spanish cattle herds were relatively small. In 1306, for example, a nobleman-rancher, Don Juan Alfonso de Benavida, owned herds of about 800 head. Some religious orders which owned ranches had larger herds. Bishko cites three Castilian nunneries with ranches: Santo Domingo de Caleruega owned about 1,000 head of cattle; Santo Domingo de Madrid boasted about 1,500 head; and Santa Clara de Guadalajara owned about 1,000 head (Bishko 1952).

Two basic types of ranching had developed in Spain by 1500 A.D. Seigneurial ranchers frequently held large grazing grounds in unpopulated areas (Bishko 1952). There is little record of restrictive legislation aimed at governing seigneurial cattle ranching. Municipal ranching, on the other hand, was governed by the local town government, which controlled the grazing land, and by the stockman's guild, or *mesta*, which administered the laws dealing with the livestock. The later medieval ordinances of Castilian and Alentejan towns regulated almost every aspect of cattle ranching: grazing rights; compensation for crop damage; wages; branding; penalties for rustling, brand-changing, or killing another man's stock; marketing and sale of cattle in the town's markets, butchershops and *ferias* (fairs), slaughtering practices; and many other related aspects of ranching. The *mesta,* managed by an elected official (the *alcade de la mesta*), supervised the *rodeo* (roundup), which occurred once or twice a year; monitored the branding of calves, the cutting out of beef for slaughter during the autumn, and the removing of strays from herds; settled ranchers' disputes; and fined or punished violators of the *mesta*'s rules. This system of regulation would be brought to the New World, and eventually to Texas.

Two categories of *vaquero* worked for the Andalusian ranchers: the freeman and the bonded servant. The freeman usually worked from one *día de San Juan* (June 24) to the next, and was paid in cash or livestock or both. Some were permitted to herd their own cattle along with those of the *ranchero*. The bonded servant was not paid a regular salary.

The *vaqueros* used dogs during roundups and while guarding the herds of cattle. Herds were tended by a foreman (*mayoral, rabadán,* or *mayordomo*) and at least three *vaqueros,* depending on the size of the herd. Larger outfits often had both a *mayoral* and a *rabadán* and perhaps a dozen or more *vaqueros.* In Andalusia, crews also had a *conocedor*—a person who memorized each cow's physical appearance to aid in detecting strays or identifying lost stock (Bishko 1952).

In sum, by the fourteenth and fifteenth centuries, ranches and landed *ganaderos* (cattle raisers) were both well established in peninsular Spain. The two systems of ranching—municipal and seigneurial—were operating, the former under the careful supervision of the *mesta.* The *vaqueros* had developed a workable system of herding cattle and conducting cattle drives over long distances. The systems of rounding up, branding, and working cattle were already well established by the time Columbus discovered the New World. When they came, the Spanish brought with them both the private and the mission systems of cattle ranching.

The Ranch in Mexico

The roots of Spanish ranching were planted in the New World on January 2, 1494, when, on his second voyage, Columbus unloaded twenty-four stallions, ten mares, and an unknown number of cattle just off the northern coast of Hispaniola, near present-day Cape Haitien, Haiti. The first of their kind to arrive in the new world, these livestock and their progeny "were destined to change the face of the New World and bring about a revolution comparable in impact to that of the Industrial Revolution nearly three centuries later" (Dary 1981). Beginning in 1498, Spaniards began to establish small cattle ranches or royal *villas* in order to increase the numbers of breeding stock. By the early 1500s, livestock raising had spread to modern-day Puerto Rico, Jamaica, Cuba, and other islands of the West Indies. Cattle eventually became so numerous that many roamed wild on the islands.

When Hernán Cortes came to Mexico in 1519, he brought with him sixteen Andalusian horses: eleven stallions and five mares. Horses would be the key factor which made it possible for Cortes to achieve the seemingly impossible—to conquer a nation of many thousands with only a few hundred men. Although some claim that these were "Arabians," the horses the Spanish brought to the New World were in reality a mixture of the greys and roans which had lived in their country for centuries and Moorish horses brought to Spain in the 1400s. As Dary notes, by 1492, "the Spaniards [in Spain] were riding the small, swift, and hardy Andalusian horses, but they had adopted Moorish saddles with short stirrups and the Moors' Arabian style of riding and fighting" (1981).

Six months before Cortes captured Mexico City, an expedition led by Gregoria de Villalobos arrived on the banks of the Pánuco River near present-day Tampico with several head of cattle—the first to arrive in Mexico. When he became lieutenant governor of New Spain less than a year later, he began coordinating the arrival of settlers, supplies, and livestock. So many cattle were being imported from the West Indies that the islanders feared they would lose their monopoly on livestock, and so imposed strong restrictions on exporting such animals to the mainland. When Cortes learned of these restrictions, he became angry. Arguing that cattle were necessary if the settlements in Mexico were to survive, Cortes persuaded Emperor Charles V of Spain to lift the restrictions placed on exportation by the islanders, and the flow of cattle and other livestock resumed.

While there were no careful records kept of the kinds of cattle brought to the New World, Rouse notes that at least three breeds of Spanish cattle were imported: (1) the *Barrenda*, or piebald, which had a white body with black markings on the neck and ears, (2) the *Retinto*, a tan and reddish colored animal with a long, narrow head, and (3) the ancient *ganado prieto*, a black animal commonly known as the Andalusian fighting bull (1977). These cattle interbred and would eventually evolve into the Texas Longhorn's ancestors a century or so later: an animal with long legs and a narrow body for covering large distances with ease, and with a mean disposition which, coupled with its weapon-like horns, could insure survival in spite of any number of enemies—man or beast. Of little use for dairy or draft purposes, longhorns were valuable only for their hides, tallow, and lean meat.

The region between Vera Cruz and Mexico City proved to be ideal for raising livestock, and the cattle population began to expand rapidly. Cortes, who established his holdings in the Mexicalzimgo Valley (south of modern Toluca), registered what was perhaps the first cattle brand in New Spain, three Latin crosses. He and other landed gentlemen made feudal vassals of the Indians in the region, taking responsibility for converting them to the Catholic faith and feeding and clothing them. In return, the Indians were to provide labor on the *ecomiendas,* or trusts. As raising cattle became more profitable, other Spaniards began grazing them on lands south and west of Mexico City. Most of these cattle wandered at will, creating problems for the Indians by destroying their crops. This style of cattle raising led to "mavericking," branding unmarked cattle with one's own brand (Dary 1981).

Cattle raisers in Mexico City attempted to resolve such problems by establishing a *mesta,* or local stockmen's organization, patterned after those in Spain. They imposed the following rules: (1) two judges of the *mesta* would call all stockmen together twice a year to find out if there were any stray animals in their herds, (2) each stock owner must have his own brand used to identify his animals, and (3) stock owners were required to register their brands, resulting in the first brand book in the New World, kept in Mexico City. Obviously, the *mesta* was a prototype for modern day stockmen's associations in Mexico and the Southwestern United States (Dusenberry 1963).

In the 1830s, a number of Spaniards acquired grazing land some distance west and northwest of Mexico City, establishing their herds in what today is southern Querétero, northern Michoacán, and southern Guanajuato. Conflict resulted when the Indians claimed ownership of the land appropriated by the Spaniards, leading to a great number of cases being filed in the court system. In response, in 1533, the Spanish government established common grazing lands some distance away from the lands under cultivation by the Indians, for the use of both groups (Morrisey 1949).

These common grazing lands, coupled with increased numbers of cattle, led to a new problem: rustling. Many of the poor, which included a large percentage of the Indian population, stole cattle and butchered them for food, hides and tallow. In an effort to protect the interests of its stockmen, the Spanish crown in 1537 extended the *mesta* and its rules throughout "New Spain." They ruled that all persons owning three hundred or more animals classified as *ganado menor* (sheep, goats, and hogs), or at least twenty animals classified as *ganado mayor* (burros, mules, horses, and cattle), were required to become members of the *mesta* and were obligated to attend or send a representative to two meetings each year (usually one in February and one in August). They were also expected to bring to the meetings any strays found in their herds, so these could be returned to their rightful owners. If the owners could not be found, the animals would be sold and the money placed in the royal treasury (Dary 1981).

The first code of the resulting large *mesta* was drawn up on July 1, 1537. It included three regulations which would serve the stockmen for forty years and would eventually be adopted north of the Rio Grande: (1) no two people could have the same brand, so that the ownership of animals could be quickly established; (2) where two stockmen happened to have the same brand, the *mesta* would assign each a distinct one; and (3) cropping the ears of animals for identification purposes was prohibited because the marks could be too easily changed (Dusenberry 1963).

The Mexican *Vaquero* Emerges

The Spanish landowners and the mission priests looked on the day-to-day working of cattle as labor beneath their dignity, so they sought others to do the work for them. Hence, the early Mexican *vaquero* was not the romantic figure the cowboy would become in American culture, but instead simply a laborer riding a horse. It is ironic that the equipment and traditions he developed over the next two hundred years would become such a vital part of the heroic cowboy image of the present.

Dary notes that the early *vaqueros'* manner of dress blended the styles worn by Spaniards with those worn by the native population. To protect himself from the sun, he wore an undecorated *sombrero* with a wide brim and a low flat crown, made of leather, woven palm fiber, or cheap felt. Under it, or tied around his neck, he sometimes wore a bandanna. He wore cotton shirts in the heat and wool shirts in the cold, although there is evidence that a few wore homemade leather shirts which were waterproof and wind resistant (1981).

By the late sixteenth century, many were wearing leather *chaquetas* (jackets) and tightfitting, knee-length breeches (*sotas*), which were usually laced up the sides. They sometimes wrapped leather leggings, or *botas*, from the knees to the ankle to protect themselves as they rode through heavy brush. Surprisingly, many rode barefooted, though some wore leather shoes with or without the heels one associates with modern-day cowboy boots. Some may have worn jackboots (military boots extending above the knee) handed down from their Spanish bosses (Dary 1981).

Strapped to whatever footwear the *vaquero* had—or to his bare feet—were a pair of large iron spurs with large rowels, often eight inches in diameter, similar to those worn by the Spanish conquistadors. This footgear had a long history. It appeared in Spain around 700 B.C. and by the fifteenth century had become a status symbol for the wealthy and powerful knights and gentlemen. Spurs came to the New World in the sixteenth century, where they, and the sounds they made, would become an important identifying marker of the *vaquero* (Dary 1981).

The earliest *vaqueros* had three styles of saddle available to them, and these they would adapt to their needs over time. The *silla de montar*, or Spanish war saddle, was heavy and cumbersome. The cantle and pommel wrapped around the rider and made it difficult for him to mount and dismount. The long stirrup leathers permitted the rider to ride with his legs in a straight position, like the knights of old. The *jineta* saddles, borrowed by the Spaniards from the Moors, were smaller and lighter, with shorter stirrups (Beatie 1981). A third style, the stock saddle, developed by Spaniards in the West Indies, was much better suited to the *vaquero*'s work. However, these were much harder to come by (Dary 1981). Over time, as the number of *vaqueros* increased, they began making their own saddles, adapting elements of the various styles.

In herding cattle, the *vaqueros* used an iron-tipped lance, or *garrocha*, similar to the one still used by *vaqueros* and cattlemen in Spain and by mounted horsemen in the bullfight rings in Mexico. During the middle of the sixteenth century, the *rodeo*, or round-up, became a common method of herding cattle. Using the lances, *vaqueros* would drive cattle from various ranches toward a specific location, where they would be sorted among the various owners (Dary 1981).

As cattle became very numerous and at the same time more valuable for their hide and tallow than for their meat, the hocking knife (*desjarretadera*, or *media luna*) became an important instrument. It consisted of a half-moon shaped blade, sharpened on the inner curve, attached to a stout pole from ten to twelve feet long. The *vaquero* would mount his horse, place the handle of the hocking knife under his arm to steady it and, holding the blade a couple of feet from the ground, urge his horse in pursuit of the animal he chose to slaughter. The sharp blade would cut the animal's hamstring, making it fall to the ground, unable to rise again. The *vaquero* struck the fallen animal behind the head with his hocking knife, severing the spinal cord. After skinning the animal, staking the hide on the ground to dry, and removing the fat to sell, he often left the flesh to rot. Existing records for 1594, which are by no means complete, indicate that some 75,000 hides were shipped to Seville, Spain, and in 1598 a fleet of ships bound for Europe carried some 150,000 cattle hides (Dary 1981).

Dary likens this process to the slaughter of bison on

Top: Typical *jacal* found in the Rio Grande Valley up into the early 1900s. The *jacal* was the home of the *peón* class. Courtesy John E. Conner Museum.

Bottom: Jacal de leña still standing on a ranch on the Mexican side of the Rio Grande. The thatched roof has been replaced with tin. Courtesy Joe S. Graham.

the Great Plains for their hides. In an attempt to prevent the depletion of the herds of cattle, the Mexican *mesta* in 1574 revised and strengthened their code. Use of the hocking knife was banned, and any person found to possess one was fined twenty pesos or received a hundred lashes in public (1981). Even though outlawed, the practice would continue for many decades, particularly along the northern frontier, where hocking knives were still used by rustlers and outlaws from both sides of the Rio Grande to raid South Texas ranches long after the coming of the Anglos.

Use of the *lazo* (lasso) or *la reata* (lariat) gradually replaced the hocking knife as the *vaquero*'s primary method of working cattle. Unlike today, however, the braided rawhide lariat of this era was not twirled above the head of the *vaquero* and then tossed over the horns or head of the chosen animal. Rather, the mounted *vaquero* placed the lariat on the end of a lance, pursued the chosen animal, and laid the loop over its head or horns. Once the lariat was in place, the *vaquero* removed the lance as the loop pulled tight. Since saddles of the era did not have saddle horns, the lariat was fastened to the cinch or other part of the *vaquero*'s saddle (Dary 1981).

Over time, the *vaqueros* developed great skill in making and using the lariat, or lasso, and by the time of the settlement of South Texas, they had achieved remarkable skills at working cattle with it on the large ranches on both sides of the Rio Grande. By the end of the sixteenth century, long cattle drives became common, as cattle were brought from the large ranches on the northern frontier to help feed the growing population in Mexico City and other cities. The *vaquero*'s skills with the lariat were important when driving large herds of cattle. They would rope the full-grown bulls and harness the troublesome ones to trained oxen, using a braided horsehair rope or halter (*cabresto*). Once broken to the trail, these bulls were useful in leading the herds (Dary 1981).

As did the cowboys driving herds of cattle northward after the American Civil War, *vaqueros* of this period worked and slept under the open skies. Some probably built lean-tos of whatever materials were at hand, since there was little opportunity to build any kind of permanent dwelling as the cattle herds moved from place to place (Morrisey 1949).

As noted earlier, the *vaquero* did not enjoy the status or adulation the American cowboy would enjoy centuries later. Most were *mestizos* (mixed Indian and Spanish ancestry), Indians, Negroes (from the many slaves brought into New Spain in the early years), and mulattoes (mixed Negro and Indian ancestry). Prior to the changes in the *mesta* code in 1574, most *vaqueros* owned their own horses and equipment—saddles, lariats, etc. In an attempt to control cattle rustling and the mass slaughter of cattle for their hides and tallow, the new code forbade non-Spaniard *vaqueros* from owning horses. The *vaqueros* had to be paid in money rather than livestock, and no one was permitted to sell livestock except the owner or his authorized representative. Spaniards who broke the law were fined fifty pesos or given a hundred lashes. A second offense doubled the penalty and led to banishment from the district where the offense had been committed. Negroes, mulattoes, *mestizos* and Indians who violated the law were treated much more severely, with punishments including the cutting off of the offender's ears for a second offense (Dary 1981).

Just as some cowboys in the Old West would become outlaws, some *vaqueros* in this period of the cattle industry in Mexico banded together and roamed the countryside, taking what they wanted. Many of these roving bands may have been the forerunners of the *bandidos* of Mexico. But the great majority of *vaqueros* were honest, hardworking men who served the *rancheros* well. Their efforts made it possible for the ranchers to prosper, pushing the cattle culture ever northward.

The Ranch Moves North

Richard J. Morrisey wrote: "The ranching frontier was the 'cutting-edge' of Spanish civilization as it pushed north. What the farming frontier was to

Anglo America, the ranching frontier was to Hispanic America" (1951).

Two major factors led to the movement of ranching culture farther and farther north. First, rich silver deposits were discovered, beginning in Zacatecas in 1546. The resulting mining communities provided a ready market for beef products—including tallow to make candles for the mines, and leather to make clothing, bags, saddles, and other objects—adding a stimulus for the ranchers who were already pushing north to take advantage of the second factor, the wide expanses of excellent grazing lands (Morrisey 1949).

As they moved north, many ranchers were given large land grants on which to graze their herds. Others simply took control of large areas of land inhabited by nomadic and often warlike Indians, who would cause major problems for not only the ranchers but the settlements and supply trains coming into the region. In response, the Spanish government established *presidios* in the region to protect the settlements and patrol the roads.

Dary provides an excellent summary of the northward expansion of the cattle industry in Mexico. He writes that the beginning of the seventeenth century was a time of depression in New Spain, and the Spanish Empire itself was in a stage of decline and decay. The mining boom of the previous century had collapsed, and the *encomienda* had failed, partly in consequence of the decline in the native population. Land became the principal source of income for the Spanish crown. Wealthy Spaniards—government officials, *encomenderos,* miners, and merchants—who already owned or claimed much of the land in New Spain, became more powerful by acquiring more and more land. As the Spanish Empire continued to suffer economically, these wealthy landowners and cattle barons began to take on responsibilities once carried by the Crown.

Until the seventeenth century, grazing rights were held in common, and one rancher couldn't legally keep his neighbors' cattle off his land. This policy changed when the Crown, in order to raise needed capital, offered to sell wealthy ranchers and other land-

owners full title to the land they already occupied. Ranchers who had seized land earlier without official sanction paid a "settlement tax" to become owners of the land and began to define the boundaries of their ranches under the *hacienda* system. Originally, the term *hacienda* was not limited to a cattle ranch, but rather any income-producing enterprise. There were lumbering *haciendas*, farming *haciendas,* mining *haciendas,* and even sheep-raising *haciendas*—as well as combinations of these.

Slowly, ranching *haciendas* began to replace the government as focal points of social, economic, and political life. As the *hacendados* (ranch owners) became more powerful, the system took a step backward toward the feudal system of Europe, since the *hacendados* basically ruled over everyone within the boundaries of the *hacienda*. The largest Mexican *haciendas* were on the northern frontier, particularly in the regions of Chihuahua, Coahuila, Nuevo León and Durango, where land was too poor to cultivate but was well suited for grazing, even though it required many acres per head of cattle. The numbers of cattle began to increase again, probably because the trade in hides and tallow had significantly declined. *Hacendados* attempted to cut expenses by lowering wages for the *vaqueros* and enforcing a system of credit at the *hacienda* store, through which many *vaqueros* became "bonded" servants to the *hacienda*. Some *vaqueros* were even born into a life of debt incurred by their fathers, and many went through life never seeing their wages, which were simply credited to their store accounts.

On the larger *haciendas,* the landowning families lived in large houses of stone or other materials. Designed to protect the owner and his family from Indian attacks, many of these houses had thick walls, high ceilings, observation towers, parapets, battlements, and narrow windows. They often had a church building near the house, and some had their own vicars. The *vaqueros* and other laborers, while at the *hacienda* headquarters, lived in very different structures. The single men shared bunkhouse quarters, and the married ones lived with their families in small huts surrounding the landowner's home. Some *haciendas* had mills for grinding corn and workshops for making wooden implements. In addition, most had large stables to care for the *hacendados'* personal horses, as well as those of the *vaqueros*. These stables had storerooms for the *vaqueros'* equipment—saddles, bridles, bits, spurs, and other riding gear (Dary 1981).

The Ranch in South Texas

Settlement of South Texas and the territory across the Rio Grande in Mexico began in the 1730s and was formally organized into the Province of Nuevo Santander in 1746. This border area had no *presidios* and few missions, so the private ranch became the primary instrument of its settlement for well over a century.

The Establishment Period: 1750–1848

The Province of Nuevo Santander was the last province to be established in the Texas-Mexico borderlands. When José de Escandón brought his 3000 settlers and 146 soldiers into the region in 1749, they were aware that the private ranch would play an important role in the settlement of this region along the Rio Grande. Many had come from the ranching areas of the provinces of Querétero, Nuevo León, and Coahuila, and they brought with them the ranching culture which would prove so important to the history of this region. They immediately adapted to this arid place and made of it a productive livestock-producing area. They brought their architectural styles, the knowledge and skills to survive in an area with few reliable sources of water, and all of the skills and equipment needed to manage large herds of livestock (Paredes 1958).

As a matter of fact, when they arrived, they discovered that the ranching frontier had arrived some twenty years earlier, as early as the 1730s, laying the groundwork for the new settlements. Ranchers from Coahuila and Nuevo León had established ranches in several places, leaving many wild cattle and horses already in the region. Escandón established three types of settlement: the *villa* (or town); the *lugar* (or settlement); and the *hacienda*. In 1749, along the south side of the Rio Grande, he established two new communities: the *villa* of Camargo on March 5 and the *villa* of Reynosa on March 14. Other communities grew out of existing ranch headquarters. For example, a ranch headquarters which had been established with nineteen families on the banks of the Alamo River and called El Paso del Cántaro, was designated by Escandón as the *lugar* of Mier on March 6, 1753, when he brought other Spanish families from Cerralvo, located about sixty miles southwest of Mier. Another ranch begun in the 1740s was designated by Escandón as the *villa* of Revilla, now Guerrero, Tamaulipas, Mexico (Graf 1942, Robertson 1985).

Other well-known towns and cities along the south side of the Rio Grande also began as ranch headquarters. For example, present-day Matamoros grew from a ranch headquarters known as San Juan de los Esteros which was established in 1765. Some thirty years later, it had grown into a community known as Congrecación del Refugio and later as Puerto (Port) del Refugio. In 1826, it was designated La Villa de Matamoros, named in honor of the soldier-priest martyred in the struggle for Mexican independence. By 1836 and the Texas Revolution, it had a population of over 7,000 inhabitants, larger than any town in what was then Texas (Lea 1957).

Within a decade, the *villas* established by Escandón had become ranching centers, including Camargo, Revilla, Reynosa, and Mier south of the Rio Grande, and Laredo and Rancho Nuestra Señora de los Dolores on the north bank (Graf 1942).

It is important to recognize that during this time period, the Rio Grande was a unifier of people, rather than the divider of nations it has become. Many ranchers ran cattle on both sides of the river, and many families who had land on the south side of the river also claimed land on the north side. Records of the General Visit of the Royal Commission to the Colonies of Nuevo Santander (1767) indicate that fifteen families to whom Escandón had given permission to settle north of the Rio Grande in 1752 had established ranches and made improvements of various types on their ranches there (Scott 1969).

Nuestra Señora de los Dolores: The First Ranch in South Texas

A brief examination of the settlement of the first ranch north of the Rio Grande provides insights into the challenges faced by early ranchers in the region. Escandón's first land grant north of the Rio Grande was given in 1750 to Don José Vásquez de Borrego, who was a successful rancher in the province of Coahuila, having established three *haciendas* in that region with over 1,300,000 acres. When he learned of Escandón's settlement of Nuevo Santander, he asked permission to settle, at his own expense, north of the Rio Grande. Escandón wanted him to settle near the Nueces River, but after exploring the area, Borrego chose to settle near the Rio Grande. Even before the grant by Escandón was officially awarded on August 22, 1750, Borrego had "staked claim" to a hundred square leagues of land, over 440,000 acres. He was willing to risk his own money to establish the ranch—the very type of settler Escandón had hoped to attract. While Escandón's original grant to Borrego was for fifty *sitios de ganado menor* (just over 98,000 acres), by the time the actual ceremony of the customary acts of posses-

sion took place on February 16, 1753, he had awarded him other grants totaling over 320,000 acres, including what is now Corralitos and the *hacienda* of San Ygnacio. It wasn't until 1767 that the land grants in Nuevo Santander were adjudicated by the Royal Commission from Mexico, and the Borrego heirs finally received the papers in 1784. The boundaries were not clearly determined, and this would lead to considerable litigation in later years. The Bourland Commission of 1852 set the size of the ranch at 276,350 acres, and this was confirmed in 1904 by the District Court of Travis County (Fish 1991).

There were three absolute requirements set forth by the Spanish government for validation of land grants: (1) homes had to be constructed on the ranch, (2) boundaries had to be marked, and (3) the land had to be stocked with animals. In addition, Borrego agreed to five other commitments: (1) the ranch would cost Escandón or the Spanish Crown nothing, (2) Borrego would provide ferry service across the Rio Grande, (3) Borrego would provide guards to protect local travelers from hostile Indians, (4) Borrego would treat the local Indians kindly, and (5) Christian instruction would be provided both for the families working on the ranch and the Indians living on the land. An extra incentive for Borrego was that he would be exempt from taxes for ten years (Fish 1991).

Nuestra Señora de los Dolores, Vásquez de Borrego's *hacienda,* became the first settlement on the northern bank of the Rio Grande below El Paso. Assuming a common social order for the typical Mexican *hacienda,* Dolores was under the supervision of a *mayordomo*—Borrego's nephew, Don Bartholome Borrego—who was in charge of the thirteen families from Borrego's Coahuila *hacienda,* San Juan del Alamo (Fish 1991).

In 1755, Escandón reported to the viceroy that the *hacienda,* whose principal industry was cattle raising, had twenty-five Spanish/Mexican families and twenty-seven Carrizo Indian families, numbering over 115 persons. (After five years, the Carrizos chose to leave the ranch and go back to their old way of life.) Borrego provided food (corn and meat), shelter, and other necessities (like clothing) for these workers. He also covered the expenses of Fray Miguel de Santa María de los Dolores of Revilla, who would spend a month of each year on the *hacienda,* teaching the Indians and Spaniards alike, baptizing and performing marriages and attending to the sick (Fish 1991).

By July 20, 1757, the José Tienda de Cuervo inspection reported the addition of twelve soldiers and one sergeant, who made up a "flying squadron" (*compania volante*) to protect the ranch from marauding Indians. Dressed in leather jackets, leather belts and shields, they were armed with pistols, muskets, swords, and daggers. They constantly patrolled the river by horseback, on the lookout for hostile Indians who raided the Dolores and other ranches from time to time during the establishment period. These were not the hunting-and-gathering Indians who had occupied the region prior to the coming of Escandón, but rather the Lipan Apaches and the Comanches from the north, who had acquired horses and become some of the most skilled warriors among the Indian tribes (Fish 1991).

The Cuervo Report also noted that the livestock on the Dolores *hacienda* included 3000 mares, 400 saddle horses, 1500 untamed mules, 100 tamed mules, 3000 head of cattle, 250 tamed donkeys and 800 untamed donkeys. Borrego was known for producing among the best mules available in the region. In addition to the fifteen *vaqueros* who tended the livestock and the thirteen men of the mounted "flying squadron," Borrego employed four men to operate the sturdy, flat ferry boats which crossed the Rio Grande. By 1755, most people who came through this region of Texas crossed the Rio Grande at Dolores (Fish 1991).

The population at Dolores had grown to forty-one families and a total population of 198 persons by 1767. These people were all living in *jacales* (small huts made of native materials such as mesquite), since none of the finer structures had yet been built for the landowning family. However, a stone chapel, or *visita,* had been constructed for holding religious services whenever the visiting priest came (Fish 1991).

There is little record of what occurred at Dolores between 1767 and the beginning of the Mexican Revo-

lution in 1810, other than the fact that Borrego had died and his descendants inherited the *hacienda.* It is known that the revolution had a profoundly negative effect on the *hacienda*'s inhabitants. The Borrego family was sympathetic to the cause of Father Miguel Hidalgo y Costillo and his quest for independence from Spain. Juan José, one of Borrego's sons who had become a priest, was executed in Chihauhua because of his open support of Father Hidalgo. In 1811, when the revolution reached the Rio Grande, a royalist officer and ten men surprised the families living at Dolores in a midnight raid. They seized and escorted to Chihauhua grandsons of the founder, Macario and Miguel Borrego, and destroyed all of the original documents at the *hacienda,* including the papers of ownership (Fish 1991).

During this era, Dolores was also under frequent attack by Indians, who killed a number of the inhabitants. In 1814, José María Margil de Vidaurri, a grandson of Borrego, built a stone tower at the ranch headquarters to defend against them. Dolores had to be abandoned in 1818 because of these frequent attacks. Vidaurri and his family moved to Laredo, where there was a small company of soldiers to protect the village.

In 1828, several citizens of Laredo declared the lands at Dolores, Corralitos, and San Ygnacio unoccupied and open to claim. The Borrego heirs appealed to the State of Tamaulipas for validation of its titles, which were restored to them. Soon afterward, Dolores was occupied again, this time with a resident *padre,* a small chapel, and a school, but the village was destroyed in the 1850s (Fish 1991). The survivors moved to Laredo and the ranch headquarters of San Ygnacio. Only seven of the forty-seven ranches in the area were occupied because of the Indian depredations. The population of Laredo had declined from a high of 2,054 in 1828 to 1,746 in 1834, and the city leaders had sent many unanswered pleas for help to Mexican authorities (Wilcox 1938).

Even though Dolores was never re-occupied, Borrego's daughter Manuela and her son José Fernando Vidaurri inherited the land. José took the grant known as the San Ygnacio subdivision; the Corralitos subdivision eventually went to his heirs; and the Dolores subdivision remained with Manuela.

In 1830, a wealthy man from the Villa de Revilla, Jesús Treviño, purchased land in the San Ygnacio subdivision. For his home, he built the structure now known as Fort Treviño. His son-in-law, Blás María Uribe, continued to build onto the structure until it was completely enclosed. When Indians raided the area, it became a refuge for neighbors, who brought their families to the fort and left their horses and wagons in the enclosed courtyard. The ranch headquarters would become the town of San Ygnacio (Fish 1991).

José Fernando Vidaurri and his wife, Alejandra Sánchez, built a house and ranch headquarters on the Corralitos subdivision. This ranch was sold in 1915 to Harvey Mecom, whose descendants still own it. Sometime after 1830, Cosme Martínez bought a large tract of the Dolores grant and established a ranch headquarters which became known as Dolores Nuevo (New Dolores), about a mile and a half north of the old *hacienda* headquarters. This new community prospered in the 1860s, but was abandoned in 1937. The site now boasts the ruins of seven stone buildings and a cemetery. Anthony Mateo Bruni, a successful Laredo businessman, purchased a large portion of the original Borrego grant and this land is still owned by his heirs (Fish 1991).

Settling a ranch in South Texas was not an easy task to be taken on by just anyone. The colonists who came with Escandón were independent, courageous people willing to risk their lives. While not all of the original land grant families had the tragic experiences of the Borregos, many did.

Other Ranches along the Texas Side of the Rio Grande

Of the original settlers in the region, fifteen families were given land grants by Escandón north of the Rio Grande in 1752. Between 1767 and 1800, a number of colonists moved north of the river, where ranching conditions were thought to be better than those in the south. Once the 1767 land grants were actually awarded, the owners were required to take possession; thus many who had lived for years in the towns of Camargo, Revilla, Reynosa, and Mier now moved onto their ranches. In many instances, the families remained in the towns where there were schools, churches, and other advantages, while the men spent certain seasons on their ranches. In other instances, the wealthy landowners remained in the villages and sent their men and cattle to the ranches (Scott 1964). Many communities today—including Laredo, Zapata, Roma/Los Saenz, Garceño, and Rio Grande City—started out as ranch headquarters on these early land grants.

In 1752, Escandón granted Captain Blás María de la Garza Falcón and his wealthy rancher father-in-law, Don Nicolás de los Santos Coy, about 433,500 acres across the river from Camargo. Within two years, there would be several large ranches operating in this area north of the Rio Grande. Captain Falcón had been a leader of Escandón's explorative expeditions in 1747, and he brought forty ranch families to settle Camargo on March 5, 1749, the first *villa* along the Rio Grande in Nuevo Santander. He named his ranch on the north banks of the Rio Grande "Carnestolendas," and he brought fifteen families to live there. Carnestolendas would later become Rancho Davis, named after the husband of one of Falcón's granddaughters, who had settled in the region. In 1848, the ranch headquarters community, which had grown with the developing riverboat trade, would be named Rio Grande City. Santos Coy, who established his ranch about nine miles up the river, named his ranch "Guardado," and he had around a hundred men altogether, working either on this or his ranch south of the river, near the San Augustín Mission. Guardado would become present-day Garceño (Scott 1969).

In 1762, Falcón pioneered the ranching settlement near the Nueces River. He brought his family and others to the ranch community which came to be known as Rancho Real de Santa Petronila, the first ranch in present-day Nueces County. By 1766, a number of other colonists had moved into the community, planting crops and tending their herds of livestock. This ranch was included in the Chiltipín Grant given to the Captain's great-grandson in 1834. By 1836, there were sixteen land grants lying partly or wholly within Nueces County, including Casa Blanca, Barranco Blanco, Rincón de los Laureles, Puentecitos, San Antonio de Agua Dulce, Padre Island, Rincón del Oso, Rincón de Corpus Christi, San Antonio del Alamo, Santa Petronila, Agua Dulce, Palo Alto, El Chiltipín, Paso Ancho de Arriba, Paso Ancho de Abajo, and San Francisco (Garcia 1984).

Back along the Rio Grande, Tomás Sánchez, a successful rancher and army veteran from Coahuila, received a land grant of some 66,000 acres to establish a ranch and *villa* at a location called Paso de Jacinto, discovered in 1745 by Jacinto de León. Since Sánchez did not have a name selected for the *villa*, Escandón suggested the name Laredo, in honor of the town in Spain located a short distance from Escandón's birthplace. The *villa* of Laredo, formally established on May 15, 1755, would eventually grow into one of the more important cities in the region (Garcia 1970).

In 1798, one of the largest landowners in South Texas was a woman, Rosa María Hinojosa de Ballí. She owned around 642,755 acres of land. Her father, Captain Juan José Hinojosa, and her husband, José María de Ballí, had applied for and received *porciones* (land grants with river front) north of the Rio Grande, and decided to apply for additional land in 1777. In 1778, the Llano Grande Grant (21,250 acres) was given to Captain Hinojosa, and the La Fería Grant (53,140.8 acres) was given to her husband. By 1790, when the grants were adjudicated, both her father and husband had died, and she inherited their land. By 1794, she had secured for her son, Juan José Ballí, the San Salvador del Tule Grant (315,319 acres) and in the name of her brother, she secured the Las Mesteñas Grant (146,670.75 acres). When she died in 1798, she left her holdings to her three sons, and by 1913, when the land was partitioned, there were more than thirty ranch settlements located within the boundaries of this property, located in Cameron, Hidalgo, and later Willacy counties (Scott 1969).

While much of the vast acreage between the Rio Grande and the Nueces River was awarded in the form of land grants by the Spanish government during its last twenty-five years of control (over 200 land grants were given), there were no *new* communities founded in the area during this period. After South Texas became part of the Mexican State of Tamaulipas in 1824 (it had been part of the Province of Tamaulipas between 1821 and 1824), the state constitution granted liberal colonization of vacant lands on the Rio Grande in an attempt to strengthen the frontier towns. In 1834, the government sold much of the land north of the Rio Grande (Graf 1942; Robertson 1985; Scott 1937).

The Search for Water

Early ranches in South Texas were established along the Rio Grande, where there was a ready supply of water for cattle and other livestock. Laying out the original land grants in a pattern called *porciones* was designed to give every landowner access to the Rio Grande. As *rancheros* began applying for land away from the river and attempting to settle on these large grants, they drew upon their cultural heritage—their ranching experience in northern Mexico—to meet the need for water for their herds of livestock.

The location of a ranch's headquarters was determined by access to adequate supplies of water. Flowing springs were a particularly valuable resource, and a number of ranch headquarters developed around the larger ones. For example, Los Ojuelos, located near a large natural spring in present-day Webb County, became the ranch headquarters for the Ysidro Gutiérrez land grant established in 1830. Other ranches were founded at the nearby springs at Las Albercas Arriba and Las Albercas Abajo. Farther north, the de la Garza Santa Gertrudis ranch headquarters, which almost half a century later would become the headquarters of the King Ranch, was established near springs on the Santa Gertrudis Creek in 1808.

Where water from rivers or from springs was not available, the early Spanish and later Mexican *rancheros* could supply water for their herds of cattle either by constructing a watering system with a *noria con buque* (well) or by building a dam across one of the many arroyos in the region. The *noria con buque* system was by far the most common, and most ranches in the arid region of South Texas had one or more of these. This watering system consisted of a large hand-dug well lined with large caliche blocks (*sillares*) or, if the ranch was within fifteen or so miles from the Rio Grande, with sandstone. Considerable knowledge and skill were required to determine where to dig the well, since the water table in this area can be fifteen hundred feet or deeper. Dug by hand with tools made by blacksmiths, some of these *norias* were round and others were rectangular (Graham 1992).

Once the well was dug and an ample supply of water discovered, the remainder of the watering system was constructed. Although there were a variety of *norias con buque* in the region, they generally consisted of a wall three to five feet high around the well with a heavy superstructure on two opposite sides. Near the top of this superstructure a large mesquite log was placed horizontally some ten or twelve feet above ground level. A large bucket, often of rawhide, would be attached to the end of a strong rope placed over the horizontal log and attached to a mule or ox, which would hoist the bucket full of water to the surface. The water was sometimes poured into large tanks made of the same caliche blocks plastered with lime mortar. The *noria con buque* at San Isidro had two large tanks, which held a total of about 6500 gallons of water, attached to a distinctively Spanish Colonial watering trough just over 100 feet long (Graham 1992).

The watering troughs of this period were commonly built with a back about five or six feet tall and the front about eighteen inches off the ground, preventing cattle from climbing into or over the trough. When a herd of cattle was brought in for water, the openings to the reservoirs were unplugged and water filled the trough. Once this herd was watered, the tanks were refilled for the next herd. Such *norias con buque* made ranching possible in much of the otherwise worthless grazing land.

Another, less-common, strategy for producing enough water for large herds of cattle was to build a *presa* (dam) across a dry arroyo, resulting in an adequate reservoir of water. One of the oldest such dams was built in the 1830s on El Randado, a ranch in the southern part of present-day Jim Hogg County. Don Hipólito García and his laborers built the dam, using equipment common in Mexico, the *mecapal* and the *guaripa*. The *mecapal* was a rawhide container carried on a man's back with a strap across his forehead, and the *guaripa* was a larger container carried by four men or skidded along the ground between two horses. In these containers, the laborers would haul dirt from the front of the dam and deposit it on the top. Cattle or oxen would be driven frequently over the freshly deposited dirt to pack it down. The dam, designed with a spillway of caliche blocks (*sillares*), usually created a reservoir of some five surface acres of water about twelve feet deep. Most ranches also had hand-dug water wells for personal consumption. The *casas mayores* (main houses), were designed with a water-collection system feeding into an underground cistern. This water was also used in some of the households on the ranch (Graham 1992).

Land Control Mechanisms

Corrals used for livestock were generally constructed of mesquite and other brush. Called *corrales de leña*, they were made of parallel mesquite posts separated by a foot or more and embedded in the ground. These parallel posts were placed in a line, from three to six feet apart. Cut mesquite trunks and branches were laid horizontally between these vertical posts to the desired height, usually from six to eight feet (Graham 1992).

These *corrales de leña* were used throughout the Establishment Period, and some are still in use today for the same basic purposes: to care for sick animals, to brand small numbers of animals (most were branded in roundups on the open range), and to break and train horses. The pens used for breaking horses were often round and very high. The horses could not see through the thick fences and therefore would not try to run through them; and given the corral's height, horses did not attempt to jump over them (Graham 1992).

The Social Order of Early Spanish Ranches

The ranch in Mexico reflected the social order of the ranch in Spain, which consisted of the landowning class and the laborer class. When the Spaniards brought the ranch to Mexico, there were not enough Spaniards of the lower social classes to work the cattle, so landowners used Indian, *mestizo,* mulatto, and Negro *vaqueros* (Dary 1981).

Encomiendas, Spanish land grants in Indian territory, had been the earliest form of ranching in Mexico. Because of the growing opposition by the Catholic Church and the Crown, however, these declined in power by 1550, to be replaced by the *estancia,* similar to the seigneural ranching of Spain. *Estancias de vacas* were privately-owned livestock ranches acquired by government grant, and they soon became the most prevalent type of ranch in Mexico, as ranching pushed farther and farther north (Dary 1981).

The ranching *hacienda* replaced the *estancia* beginning in the early 1600s, well after the *vaquero* had become a common figure in Mexican cattleraising. By this time, although much of the land was still owned by wealthy Spaniards—government officials, miners, merchants, and individual clergymen—and by the Catholic Church, the Spanish Empire was experiencing a time of depression. As the Crown's power declined in Mexico, the wealthy landowners began taking on the responsibilities once shouldered by Spain's representatives. To make money, the Spanish government began to sell to the wealthy landowners full title to the land they occupied, making it possible to define the specific boundaries of their property. Eventually, as Dary writes, "The *hacendado* ruled everyone within the boundaries of his *hacienda.* He was a lord and chief agent of local government. He created a world to his own liking" (1981). Fish, writing of the Dolores *hacienda* of Vásquez de Borrego, stated that "the organization of the *hacienda* was along military lines and was highly authoritarian. The social structure closely resembled a feudal estate. . . ." (1991).

Such was the *hacienda* which found its way to South Texas and persisted until well after the end of the Establishment Period. There were two distinct social classes, the *patrón* (landowning class)—some, but not all, of which were *hacendados*—and the *peón* (working class), which consisted of *vaqueros* and laborers.

Based on her interviews with ranch people born before 1850, Jovita González (1930) described the social structure on South Texas ranches. She emphasizes that the *patrón* was considered advisor and counselor, as well as judge and jury, for the *peones.* But he also protected them in times of danger. He or his chosen *mayordomo* supervised the various kinds of work on the ranch, from planting crops or building dams to caring for the cattle.

The *peón* and his family lived in a small one-room *jacal* with a thatched roof and a dirt floor. The walls were made of whatever materials were readily available, but were always supported by four corner posts, forked at the top and buried solidly in the ground. The ridgepole of the thatched roof was also supported by tall posts embedded in the ground and forked at the top. The one room served as both living room and bedroom. The kitchen, separate from the *jacal,* often consisted of a small enclosure or a *ramada* (arbor) made of grass or corn stalks, with a small space nearby as a dining area. Usually an *olla* (earthen pot) hung from one of the rafters of the *ramada,* covered with canvas or cloth soaked in water and serving as the water cooler for the home (Graham 1991c).

The furniture was usually homemade. The bed might be four posts embedded in the dirt floor with a frame and boards covered with a grass mattress. Other furniture might include a few chairs and a table, with a mirror hanging on the plastered, whitewashed interior wall. Every home, regardless of how humble, had an *altarcito,* a small altar which boasted a statue or picture of the Virgin de Guadalupe or another saint, surrounded by paper flowers or candles. Some altars were larger and more complex, with more statues, paintings and decorations. Around this place of honor, the mother taught her children the various Catholic prayers and rites.

The *peón* laborer did whatever work was necessary around the *hacienda*—planting and harvesting, herding goats, digging wells, building dams and houses. He was not permitted to own any property, but often kept a goat, pig, or a few chickens in the enclosure around his house. His wife might plant a few rows of corn or beans or a few pumpkin vines in back of the *jacal*. Since the *peón* had only rare opportunities to travel to town, he spent his small wage or credit in the ranch general store, building up a debt which increased in times of illness, family deaths, marriages, or other such life experiences (González 1930).

If the *peón* and his family wished to travel to another ranch or town, he was dependent on the *patrón* for a wagon or ox-cart. In times of illness, the doctor could not be summoned without the *patrón*'s permission. The *peón* also consulted with the *patrón* in such personal matters as the marriage of his children; if the *patrón* approved, he would serve as the *portador,* the one who would ask for the girl's hand in marriage for the *peón*'s son. This kind of dependency created a strong bond between the *patrón* and his *peones*.

The *vaquero,* on the other hand, was much more independent. Often a *mestizo* or son of a *criollo* (Spaniard born in the New World) landowner with meager land holdings, he did not consider himself bound to any *patrón.* He felt that one day, if given the opportunity, he might become a landowner himself, perhaps through marriage (González 1930).

Most of the social events on the ranch, particularly the celebrations, were also separated by social class. The *peónes* (including the *vaqueros*) enjoyed dances from time to time, and these would last from dusk until dawn, after which they would go about their normal work day. They also celebrated holidays such as New Year's day, the feast of *el día de San Juan, el día de Santiago,* or the day of the Holy Innocents. The latter celebrations often included dances, speeches, storytelling, and such *vaquero* sports as *correr el gallo,* a game which tested the horsemanship skills of the riders. The music was usually provided by a guitar, a violin, and an accordion (González 1930).

The *patrón* class lived in the *casas mayores* on the ranch, made of carved sandstone (if the ranch was within about fifteen miles of the Rio Grande) or *sillares,* where stone was not available. Up until the 1860s, these houses were fortresses against Indian attacks, usually with high, flat ceilings and roofs of *chipichil* (a mortar made of lime, sand and gravel) which would not burn. These roofs were supported by huge *vigas* set across the tops of the walls. The floors were often made of *chipichil* also, although flat stones were common too. At each end of the house and on each side of the doors and windows would be *troneras,* or gunports, through which the ranchers could shoot at attackers (Graham 1992).

The main house usually consisted of two or three large rooms, although some *casas mayores* were considerably larger. The main room was a large *sala* where the family gathered in the evening, or where guests were entertained. This was often decorated with animal skins, mounted deer heads, powder horns and muskets adorning the walls. Adjoining this room was another, often the main bedroom, where the wife sometimes entertained her guests. Children slept here until they grew older, at which time the boys were often moved into the men's quarters in a nearby building and the girls were given their own bedrooms in the main house.

The furniture in these homes was the best that could be bought in Monterrey, Matamoros, Laredo, and later Brownsville. It was not uncommon to find large hand-carved beds with elegant canopies and silk draperies. Dressers and tables often boasted marble tops. Family portraits and handmade objects of various types decorated the walls. One could find beautiful works of *deshilado* (drawn work), weaving, and quilting adorning these homes (González 1930).

The kitchen was often a thatched-roofed *jacal* structure with a dirt floor, separate from the main house, although it was a part of some *casas mayores.* Either way, the fire in the huge *chimenea,* a fireplace about three feet above the floor—which made it possible to cook while standing—could make it unbearably hot in the long summer months. Usually the cooking was done by the wives and daughters of the *peónes,* who used the copper pots, iron skillets and utensils which often hung from pegs on the walls on either side of the *chimenea.* The huge *horno,* or oven, was built outside. It was dome shaped, and varied in size. Hot coals were used to heat it for cooking various foods made of corn, flour, or meat (Graham 1992).

Amusements for the *patrón* class reflected the traditions of its wealthy Spanish and Mexican forebears. When families from nearby ranches visited, the men and women gathered into separate groups to talk and to enjoy one another's company. The men also engaged in races, cock-fights, gambling and dancing. The best race horses in the region (both Texas and Mexico) were brought to these celebrations, and large sums of money were wagered on races, as well as at gaming tables (González 1930).

Dances given by the ranch owners were the social events of the year. They were the only form of amusement shared by men and women of the landed aristocracy. Ladies, glad for the opportunity to show their finest apparel and charms, arrived in family coaches escorted by mounted riders. Music for these dances was provided by orchestras, which played mostly waltzes, polkas, and schottisches. The dance was often followed by a midnight dinner, where fine wines were drunk and toasts offered (González 1930).

There were clear gender roles in this early Spanish and Mexican society. Women in both social classes had similar roles within their own families. They were homemakers, spiritual guides, and healers; in addition, among the *patrón* class, they were responsible for their children's educations. The *dueña* (*patrón*'s wife) had women from the *peón* class to help with much of the housework. While *peón* women might have work assigned to them on the *hacienda*, their primary task was to care for their own families. As homemakers, they cleaned house; prepared the meals; tended the garden, chickens or domestic animals; made clothing; cared for the children, and made various decorative objects for the home (Graham 1985, González 1930).

Inasmuch as medical doctors were scarce in the region, even people on the large ranches had limited access to their services. Both social classes relied primarily on folk medicine passed from generation to generation by word-of-mouth or example. Common ailments—headaches, stomach aches, and fevers—as well as more serious illnesses, were treated with *remedios caseros* (household remedies) made from a wide variety of medicinal herbs, many of which continue

to be popular in the twentieth century. Of particular interest are the various "folk illness syndromes" prevalent in the region which are not recognized by today's medical experts. These include *susto,* an illness common to children and caused by extreme fright; *empacho,* caused by blockage of the digestive system; *mal de ojo,* a childhood illness caused by an adult looking at them in excess admiration; and *caída de la mollera,* or fallen fontanel, when the soft spot of an infant's head sinks in too far, thought to be caused by jarring, bumping, or dropping a child. It was not unusual for a mother who diagnosed her child as having one of these illnesses to seek assistance from one of the local healers, even if she was familiar with the appropriate ritual treatments. Medical care at this level was almost exclusively the domain of women (Graham 1985).

Parteras (midwives) delivered most of the children, having learned childbirthing skills through apprenticeships. Bad bruises, sprains, or even broken bones were treated by the *sobador(a)*, a folk chiropractor who relied extensively on massaging. Much rarer was the *curandero(a)*, the folk healer par excellence, who not only knew the many medicinal herbs and the various ritual cures, but could treat major life-threatening illnesses as well. Thought to have received a *don de Díos* (gift from God) to heal the sick, they were the only ones believed capable of curing cases of illness caused by *brujería,* or witchcraft. Don Pedrito Jaramillo, who lived on the Los Olmos Ranch in Brooks County, was for years the best-known *curandero* in South Texas. He had a large following until his death in 1907. Many people still seek his healing powers by visiting the shrine built over his grave near Falfurrias (Graham 1985).

Most ranches were visited only once a year by the missionary priests (usually Oblates in South Texas) sent from the communities along the Rio Grande to hold mass and perform the various rites and ceremonies—baptisms, *quinceañeras* (the coming-of-age celebration for young women when they turned fifteen years of age), weddings, and sometimes funerals. One such priest was Father Joseph Marie Closs (known as Father José María), who for fifty years served as priest, physician, and advisor to many ranching families in the Roma region, where his parish was located. He died at the age of eighty, still an excellent rider (González 1930).

The priest's visits were times of celebration. The *patrones, vaqueros,* laborers and their families would come from surrounding ranches. Preparations would be made days in advance—bread and cakes baked; coca beans roasted, ground and made into chocolate squares; a cow or calf butchered; chickens dressed; and unused quilts and mattresses aired in the sunlight. Servant women stayed busy grinding corn on the *metate* for tortillas or washing linen cloths to be used on the altar. It was an important opportunity for young people to meet others of the opposite sex, and perhaps begin a courtship (González 1930).

Many of the larger *haciendas* had chapels, called *visitas,* reserved for the priests. These chapels would have a large altar, homemade benches, and some also had handmade confessionals. The altars frequently had icons, carvings or paintings of various saints who were important to the ranch owners, although the Virgin of Guadalupe was the most common figure here as well as at home.

If there was no chapel on the ranch, the *dueña* would invite the priest to use the altar in the main house for rites and ceremonies. These homemade altars provided the women an opportunity to show their artistic skills. On one end of the main *sala,* or living room, she (and the other women helping her) would hang a large white sheet, decorated with ribbons—red, yellow, orange, blue, etc. Sprays of cedar, oleander and handmade paper flowers would be placed around the altar, which would have as its focus the pictures of saints and angels, along with wood and marble statues of favorite saints, most handcarved (González 1930).

Near dusk, while the folk from nearby ranches were still arriving, the priest would wait in the patio or other secluded place. After the evening meal, everyone would gather before the altar to recite the Rosary and to hear the *padre's* message. Together, male and female voices would be raised in praises, prayers, and thanks to the Mother of God.

O, María, Madre mía	O Mary, Our Mother,
O, Consuelo del mortal	Consolation of all mortals,
Amparadme y guiadme	Protect us and guide us
A la patria celestial.	To our celestial home.

During the remainder of the year, in the absence of a priest, it was considered the woman's role to teach her children religious doctrine and to lead the family in prayer before the altar (González 1930).·

Another important role for women of the *patrón* class was to see to the education of their children. This was not difficult for the very wealthy, who frequently sent their children to schools in Mexico, such as those in Monterrey or Saltillo. Ranchers of moderate wealth put their children into private schools in communities along the border. If neither of these was an option (or in some cases, if the parents chose), the children would be educated at home. As a general rule, children of the *peón* class did not attend school, as most *patrónes* discouraged the practice (González 1930).

A final difference between the two social classes can be seen in the separate ranch cemeteries, one for the *patron's* family and the other for the *peones'* families. Crosses in the latter were almost always handmade of wood, iron, and later cement. The *patron's* marker—and often a mausoleum—would be constructed by skilled craftsmen using the best materials available. Both types of cemetery are depositories of religious folk art in the region.

The *Vaqueros*: *Their Skills and Equipment*

As had been the case in Spain, *vaqueros* of the new world were of the poorer social classes—Indians or *mestizos* early on, and later perhaps *criollos,* whose parents were small landowners. While the Mexican *vaquero* borrowed some components of his costume and equipment from his Spanish predecessors, along with some of the skills of working cattle, he played a key role in developing many of these into the forms known in the twentieth century.

The first costume of the Mexican *vaquero* was basically whatever he had when he began his work. One of the few descriptions of the *vaquero* of the 1800s was given by Captain George W. Hughes, who was with General Wool on his march from San Antonio to Saltillo, Mexico. He wrote:

Fancy to yourself a rather light-colored Indian dressed in a pair of leather unmentionables, without suspenders, buttoning from the knee downwards, which are usually left open in warm weather for comfort, and to exhibit the white drawers underneath; a common cotton shirt; a red sash tied tightly around the waist; a pair of sandals on his feet, and enormous iron spurs on heel; with a heavy conical felt hat (that could almost resist a sabre cut) on the head, and a long iron-pointed aspen goad in hand, and you have a perfect picture of the ranchero, or rather *vaquero*. Mounted on a spirited pony, with a lasso at his saddle-bow, he is no mean adversary for a single man to encounter. He rides well and fearlessly, and throws the lasso with unerring aim. It is a beautiful sight to see him with his old blanket (worn as a poncho in cold weather) streaming in the wind, his head bent eagerly forward, and lasso whirling in circles high in the air, chasing down some refractory animal that he seldom fails to catch, at the first throw, by the neck or hind foot, bringing him violently to the ground. . . . It is amusing to see the young urchins following the example of their elders, practising [sic] on little pigs and tender kids, who by no means appear to enjoy the fun. . . . Every Mexican, whatever his condition may be, is expert with the lasso, and the throwing of it may be regarded as the national amusement. (George W. Hughes, Memoir Descriptive of a Division of the United States Army, under the command of Brigadier General John E. Wool, from San Antonio de Bexar, in Texas, to Saltillo, in Mexico, Sen. Ex. Doc. No. 32, 31st Cong., Last Sess., p. 41)

La reata, one of the most vital pieces of the *vaquero*'s equipment, evidently developed in the New World rather than in Spain. As the *vaqueros* in Mexico became more proficient with its use, they discovered that the lariat had advantages over the hocking knife. They could use it to capture cattle to brand them or check their brands. Over time, *vaqueros* developed great skills in the use of the lariat, so that by the time they arrived in Texas, they had perfected its use. By then the *vaquero* saddle, with its large saddle horn, was almost universal among the *vaqueros*. When branding, the *vaqueros* would rope an animal and *darle vuelta,* or wrap the lariat quickly around the saddle horn. The English word for this process is to "dally." The animals to be driven to market were branded on the shoulder with a brand called *el fierro para ventear* (the brand for selling), later called a "trail brand" by Anglo ranchers. Permanent brands on cattle remaining with the rancher were placed on the hip (Dary 1981).

Early lariats were made of rawhide, braided with four, six, eight, or twelve strands. The cowhide would be pegged to the ground until it was dry, at which point the *vaquero* would take a sharp knife and, working from the outside of the hide, cut it into one long, thin strip. He would then use the knife to shave the hair from the strand of hide. When he had enough of these strands for a lariat of adequate length (in early Texas that would have been a hundred or so feet), he would wet the strips, stretch them, wet them again, and braid them to form a lariat about as thick as a man's little finger. The lariat became the *vaquero*'s most important tool for handling cattle.

Vaqueros in Spain had developed the skills of conducting roundups, long cattle drives, and marking and branding livestock. These skills were also essential to cattle raising in New Spain. By the 1650s there were regular cattle drives from the frontier regions to markets in Mexico City and other population centers. *Vaqueros* would help drive herds of several thousand to these markets or to new pasture lands along the northern frontier (Dary 1981). These same skills would be used by ranchers in South Texas, who drove large herds of cattle to the interior of Mexico and east to Louisiana, well over a century before the great cattle drives to northern markets following the Civil War (Graf 1942).

Roundups were conducted twice a year, once in the spring and once in the fall. *Vaqueros* from local ranches would drive all of the cattle from various directions to a specified location, where they would brand the calves with whatever brands the mothers bore, and separate strays for returning to their proper owners (Ramírez 1979).

During most of the year, when not engaged in roundups or cattle drives, the *vaqueros* lived in camps on the open range, moving with the herds from place to place. They built crude lean-to shelters near water and wood, where they cooked their own food, usually *atole* (a corn meal mush), beef or wild game, and *pinole,* which is a powder made of toasted corn ground on a *metate* and mixed with cinnamon and sugar or *piloncillo* (Dary 1981).

Laws Regulating the Cattle Industry

As a consequence of the incredibly rapid growth of the cattle industry in Mexico, the *mesta* code of 1537 was revised in 1574, and in this form it regulated cattle raising in South Texas until December 23, 1823, when the assembly of Nuevo Santander (soon to become the state of Tamaulipas) passed a law governing the holding of *corridas de caballada mesteñas* (roundups to capture wild cattle and horses) between the Rio Grande and the Nueces River. To hold a *corrida,* one had to get a license from the governing body wherever the *corrida* was to be held, and warn the neighboring ranchers so that they could join in. Only ranchers or those who had grazed stock on the lands could get a license, and they had to file reports after the roundup. Cattle already branded were delivered to their owners, and the remainder belonged to those who found them, after paying the local *ayuntamiento* (local government) two *reales* for each head. These roundups could be held only between October 11 and December 31 each year, a law which remained in effect until 1831 (Graf 1942).

Spanish-Mexican Contributions to the U.S. Cattle Industry

By the end of the Establishment Period of the ranch in South Texas, the elements of ranching, having evolved over eight centuries, were securely in place. Ranches in the northern Mexican states, which were larger than any in the United States at that time, introduced the knowledge and skills to transform dry, arid lands into productive ranches that would one day help to feed large populations. With the ranch came the highly skilled *vaquero* and his cattle-working techniques —including branding, ear marking, seasonal roundups, cattle roping, long cattle drives, the problems of cattle

rustling and the laws designed to end it, and the technique called "brush popping" (chasing cattle through shrubs and thorny brush). He also brought his equipment, including the *vaquero* saddle, the rawhide lariat, the braided horsehair rope (*cabresto*), the *garrocha,* the branding iron, *chappareras,* the bridle bits and reins, hackamores (*jácimas*), spurs, and the *vaquero*'s costume (Graham 1991b).

Challenges to Early Ranchers

Ranching was a way of life in early South Texas, but it was by no means idyllic. Those who chose to live on the *haciendas* faced the threat of violence from two different sources: Indians and Anglo Texans. Indians, understandably hostile at their loss of territory, constantly raided ranches in the region from the late 1700s until 1872, the year of the last documented Indian raid of a ranch in South Texas. Warlike tribes from the north—particularly the Comanches and the Lipan Apaches, who had acquired horses and become skilled horsemen—proved a major threat to ranchers. The ranchers living closer to the Rio Grande, who could escape to Reynosa, Mier, Revilla, Camargo, and Laredo, were safer from Indian attacks than were those living great distances from the river. Those living far from these villages were at the mercy of the Indians.

During the first decade of the 1800s, for instance, the Dolores *hacienda* suffered a number of Indian raids and many of its inhabitants were killed. In 1814, a tower was built there in an effort to protect the settlers, but four years later, Dolores had to be abandoned because of the intensity of the attacks. It was re-occupied in 1830, but destroyed completely in the 1850s. Still, the last recorded murder by Indians in Zapata County occurred on the Dolores lands in 1888. Alejandro Vidaurri, Jr., was killed while herding cattle on the northern section of the grant (Fish 1991).

At one time in the 1840s, only seven of the forty-seven ranches in the Laredo area were occupied because of the threat of Indian attacks. Even the inhabitants of the villa of Laredo were not immune to the warlike Indians. In spite of many strong pleas to the Mexican officials, Laredo never received military

Left: Jacal de leña (mesquite *jacal*) along the Rio Grande in the early twentieth century. Walls and thatched roofs were supported by *horcones* (corner posts) set vertically into the ground. Courtesy John E. Conner Museum.

Below: Stone ranchhouse. This *casa mayor* was built in the 1840s at Rancho San Francisco in Zapata County. Note the stone *bancas* around the house and the *troneras* (gunports) by each door and in the center of the facing wall. The hipped tin roof was added in the 1950s to protect the house from damage which could be caused by heavy rains in the area. Courtesy Joe S. Graham.

Top: This is an inside view of a *tronera* (gunport) common in the *casas mayores* throughout South Texas into the 1860s. Courtesy Joe S. Graham.

Bottom: This is a view of the exterior opening of a *tronera* in the main house on Rancho San Francisco in Zapata County, built in the 1840s. Courtesy Joe S. Graham.

Two-story Spanish colonial main house. This *casa mayor* is
made of *sillares* (caliche blocks), quarried from beneath the
topsoil. Courtesy John E. Conner Museum.

Right: Interior wall of a hand-dug well at Randado. Nearly 90 feet deep, it was lined with *sillares* (caliche blocks) down to the caliche base. Courtesy Joe S. Graham.

Below: Noria con buque (hand-dug water well for watering livestock) on the Los Olmos Ranch in Southern Duval County. Dug in the 1850s, it is lined with caliche blocks. Courtesy Joe S. Graham.

Facing page, top: Early hand-dug well on Mota de Olmos Ranch in Duval County lined with *sillares* (caliche blocks). Wells like this were the primary source of water for people living on early South Texas ranches. Courtesy Joe S. Graham.

Facing page, bottom: Cistern at Villa Nueva, Mexico. A hand-dug cistern was part of a water collection system designed to save rainwater for household use. This was necessary where surface water was brackish or heavily mineralized. Courtesy Joe S. Graham.

A *corral de leña* in Zapata County, the only common ranch enclosure during the colonial and Mexican periods in South Texas. They were used for capturing, breaking and training horses, and working various kinds of livestock. Courtesy Joe S. Graham.

protection. Between 1828 and 1834, the population of Laredo declined from 2,054 people to 1,746 (Wilcox 1938). In a letter written to the Governor of Tamaulipas on December 21, 1835, the *alcalde* of Laredo wrote:

. . . the incursions of the barbarous Indians continue with all the vigor and force customary. Fifteen days ago today they killed citizen Ramón de la Garza at his ranch, and stole a considerable number of horse stock; and only six days ago they killed at a place called Rio Frio on the road to Béxar . . . Gregorio Canales and Luciano Benavides. (Laredo Archives, letter, Ildefonso Ramón, *alcalde,* to governor of Tamaulipas, dated Laredo, December 21, 1835)

That year, these warlike Indians killed twenty-six people in the Laredo area and stole over 1000 head of livestock (Wilcox 1938).

The other factor which made life on ranches in South Texas very hazardous was the Texas Revolution of 1836. Although the southern boundary of the Province of Texas was the Nueces River, Texans claimed the Rio Grande River as the boundary. This argument was not settled until the Mexican-American War and the Treaty of Guadalupe Hidalgo. Between 1836 and 1848, many of the ranch owners left their land and moved to the communities along the Rio Grande, fleeing the dangers of Anglo bandits in the region. In September, 1839, Lieutenant Browne of the Texas Army reported to the Adjutant General:

When I arrived in Victoria I found it filled with a set of men who have given themselves the title of a *band of Brothers*. . . . They are all in the cow stealing business, and are scattered all over this frontier. They pretend . . . they steal only from the enemy; but I am convinced, to the contrary, that they steal from Texans as well as Mexicans. . . . [One said to me] that he was one of the band of Brothers and wished me to know that they could defend themselves against any force the government could send to oppose them. . . . I am convinced that there are no less than three or four hundred men engaged in this business. . . . One of them told me that they had their expresses better regulated than any regular army that has ever been in the country. (Fugate 1961)

Faustino Morales, a *vaquero* on the Kenedy Ranch in the 1880s, recalled having witnessed Anglo outlaws from Corpus Christi attacking Mexican ranches, burning their buildings and killing or driving the Mexican ranchers away. He states that "there were many small ranches belonging to Mexicans, but then the Americans came in and drove the Mexicans out and took over the ranches" (Villarreal 1972).

From El Rancho to The Ranch, 1848–1885

Many of the Anglo Americans who settled in South Texas before the Mexican American War and the Treaty of Guadalupe Hidalgo in 1848 were single men who subsequently married into Mexican families, adopted the Mexican culture, and for all practical purposes become Mexicans. These Anglos brought with them the values and technologies which would make significant changes in the 800-year-old institution of the private cattle ranch. Others came in as businessmen, working the river trade in boats along the Rio Grande. These new arrivals included men like Charles Stillman, Richard King, Mifflin Kenedy, John Young, and John Allen. The latter three married into landed families in the region.

These men saw the importance and value of ranching as a source of income and began purchasing land grants from Mexicans, many of whom had little use for the lands lying some distance from the Rio Grande because of the Indian troubles of the time. The Mexican landowners with property close to the river were more reluctant to sell, and much of this land still belongs to their descendants.

The Treaty of Guadalupe Hidalgo declared the land between the Rio Grande and the Nueces Rivers as American soil, causing a significant increase in the number of Anglo Americans who came to the area. During this period of time, over eighty percent of the land in South Texas changed hands (De León 1979). Although many original landowning families willingly sold their land because of Indian raids, constant warring with the Anglos, and the turmoil of facing new laws, a new legal system, and a new official language, others became victims of the newcomers—some from Mexico but most from the United States—who bought by deception, took by force, and otherwise dispossessed the original families of their land. Some families were actually killed when they refused to sell or leave their lands.

Unscrupulous law enforcement officers and judges took advantage of the Mexicans' lack of understanding of the new American laws. A copy of court records in Brooks County shows one example of the sale of 5000 acres of land for $15 in delinquent taxes. The deed of the Armstrong Ranch in Jim Hogg County shows the sale of 4,431 acres of land for $8.31 back taxes (copy of deed in possession of author). A Mexican American lost it and an Anglo bought it.

This transition period was also marked by an unprecedented rise in cattle rustling and raids on ranches, both by Mexican thieves who drove Texas cattle to Mexico (or butchered them for their hides) and Anglo thieves who raided Mexican and Anglo ranchers on both sides of the Rio Grande. Although outlawed in Mexico over three centuries before, the hocking knife came into use again in South Texas during this period of lawlessness. Thieves immobilized the cattle with these knives, then killed and skinned them before hauling the hides to market.

This problem continued until the Texas Rangers began imposing order in South Texas in 1875 and Porfirio Díaz was elected President of Mexico in 1876. Díaz and his government imposed control on the Mexican side of the border, as the Rangers did for the Texas side. In 1876, Ranger Captain McNelly reported that there was an organized band of desperadoes between Goliad and the Nueces River, numbering from four to five hundred, who lived by robbing others. They often divided into bands of twenty-five to forty men, forming settlements in different counties in the area (Smith 1986). By 1880, thanks to the combined efforts of Texas and Mexico, the extensive cattle thievery and killings had ended, and relative peace was established.

From a Way of Life to a Business

Contrary to popular notions, the Anglo *adopted* rather than *invented* ranching. Their coming to South Texas did, however, initiate a number of changes to the ranching tradition. The 1850 census of Nueces County indicates that the Anglos were at first farmers and woodsmen rather than ranchers. Those who wanted to try ranching had to rely on Mexican traditions, particularly the vast store of knowledge of the Mexican *vaqueros*. This confluence of cultures brought changes in the ranch which transformed it from what was principally a way of life into a profit-making enterprise. The exchange of information and tradition was by no means one-way; while the Anglos were learning from the *mexicanos*, the *mexicanos*, in turn, were learning from the Anglos.

The first large land purchases by Anglos came in 1839 and 1844, *before* the Treaty of Guadalupe Hidalgo, but neither sale resulted in the establishment of a ranch. The first large Anglo-owned ranches in the region were those established by Mifflin Kenedy, Richard King, Major James H. Durst, F. J. Parker, and W. G Hale (Lea 1957).

In 1852, Kenedy attempted to ranch at Valerio on the Nueces River, and in 1854 he bought land on the huge San Salvador del Tule grant, some sixty miles northwest of Brownsville, but he did not attempt to stock it. In 1853, Richard King and his partner Gideon "Legs" Lewis (a former Texas Ranger captain who had a print shop, a real estate business and a mercantile store in Corpus Christi) bought the Rincón de Santa Gertrudis grant, originally the property of Juan Mendiola of Camargo. Until his death in 1836, Mendiola had a house, pens, and livestock on the land, but the ranch had been abandoned because of the Texas Revolution. Paying $300 for 15,500 acres, King received a warranty deed from Mendiola's heirs on July 25, 1853 (Lea 1957).

In 1854, he and Lewis purchased the de la Garza Santa Gertrudis grant, consisting of 53,000 acres. Lewis was killed a year later, so it was King, Kenedy and James Walworth who formed a company called R. King & Company in 1860, with about 20,000 head of cattle and some 3,000 head of horses. Just two years later, the company bought more than 90,000 acres of the Laureles grant from Charles Stillman and also some 22,000 acres of the William Mann ranch property in the Casa Blanca grant north of the Santa Gertrudis. When Walworth died in 1865, King and Kenedy dissolved the company and paid Walworth's wife $50,000 for his part. In an 1868 division of property, Kenedy took the Laureles land, while King received the remainder. In 1882, Kenedy sold the Laureles grant and all his livestock for $1,100,000 to a syndicate from Dundee, Scotland—the Texas Land and Cattle Company, Ltd. A month later, he organized the Kenedy Pasture Company on land of the La Parra grant, a ranch which continues today (Lea 1957).

Another major land purchase took place in 1852, the year Kenedy first bought land. Major James H. Durst, a wealthy landowner and merchant from East Texas, bought the majority of the La Barreta land grant (92,996.4 acres) from the Ballí family for 1600 pesos. He never moved onto the land, which had no cattle, fences, buildings, modern water wells or tanks by the time he died six years later. His daughter and son-in-law moved onto the property in 1885, establishing the 50,000-acre Armstrong ranch in present-day Willacy County. In the early 1850s, F. J. Parker and W. G. Hale bought the Santa Rosa grant (about twenty-five miles south of the Santa Gertrudis of Richard King) and hired a manager to live on the ranch and work it (Smith 1986).

Several ranchers from Mexico also moved into the area. Rancho La Mota de Olmos was established in southern Duval County by the Bazáns, a ranching family from Camargo. They built traditional flat-top homes of *sillares* with *chipichil* roofs and floors, *corrals de leña,* and hand-dug wells to water their cattle. A bit farther to the northeast, the Hinojosa family established the El Guajillo ranch, beginning in the 1850s. It grew to some 60,000 acres, and much of it still belongs to the descendants of the original owner. As at Mota de Olmos, the Hinojosas built homes and corrals, as well as a fairly large earthen dam.

When Richard King decided to buy cattle in Mexico

to stock his Santa Gertrudis ranch in 1854, he did something else which set a precedent for the way Anglo ranches would be run during this period in ranching history. While in Mexico, he offered to settle an entire community at the Santa Gertrudis ranch, promising the *vaqueros* twenty-five *pesos* a month, food and shelter. Over one hundred men, women, and children (including Damon Ortíz, whom King hired to take care of the *remuda*), came to the ranch to work for him, bringing all of their belongings in two-wheeled *carretas* (Lea 1957). This established what was essentially a *hacienda*, with its class structure equivalent to that institution's two distinct social classes—the *patrón* and the *peón* (Lea 1957).

King had originally planned to be an absentee landlord and live in Brownsville with his family. As he got more interested and involved in the ranch and its work, he decided to move to the ranch headquarters, which he and Lewis had put together as a cow camp with a primitive shelter sometime between September 1, 1852, and March 13, 1853. The King family lived in a *jacal* while the main house was being built, just as the early Spanish and Mexican *hacendados* had done. The house the Kings eventually moved into, built of cut lumber hauled from Corpus Christi, was made in the typical Anglo style of the time. For his workers, King provided houses, water, and specific amounts of food based on the number of children in the family. As on earlier *haciendas,* the King Ranch had its own store, where the workers bought most of their needs. By 1885, the ranch employed about 300 men, and by 1895, they branded some 30,000 calves. By the time of his death in 1885, King had acquired about 640,000 acres in South Texas. The King Ranch people became known as *los Kineños,* the King People, and this basic system of relationships continued until 1971 (Lea 1957).

This experience emphasizes an important point made by Jovita González: because of the history of distinct separation of the two social classes, the *peón* class, including the *vaqueros,* was as happy working for Anglo landowners as they had been for Spanish or Mexican ones (1930). There is nothing to indicate that King reduced his workers to vassals through debt, but there is no question that his workers were very loyal to their *patrón* and his family and that they were proud to be *los Kineños*. Just as important is the fact that King relied on his *vaqueros* for their knowledge of raising cattle and training cowhorses. As Lea has noted, King planned to adopt the Mexican system of ranching, improve it, and make it pay (1957). This he did.

With the Treaty of Guadalupe Hidalgo, Anglo laws governing land ownership replaced the Mexican laws and Spanish traditions of earlier periods. In Spain, land (and other wealth) was passed from one generation to the next through primogeniture, a system in which the oldest son inherited all of the family's wealth, thus insuring that it would remain intact. The younger males in the family sought their livelihoods in the military, in commerce, and sometimes in the church as priests. By the time the colonists arrived in South Texas, this system had been modified somewhat. The family wealth was held in common—as a *herencia,* or inheritance—with each member of the family having certain *derechos,* or rights. But the property remained intact, and one individual could not take his part of the property and go his own way. Under the new Anglo law, an individual could go to court and sue for his part of the inheritance and then either establish his own ranch or sell the property to someone else. Over time, this resulted in the division of the large ranches, even those which had been successful, into smaller and smaller units (Montejano 1987).

Another reason that, prior to the coming of the Anglos, the ranch was more a way of life than a profit-oriented business was the fact that there was no ready market for the large numbers of cattle a rancher could raise. A few ranchers had made drives into Louisiana in spite of the Spanish and Mexican governments' attempts to restrict trade there. Some also made cattle drives south into Mexico, even though it already had a large supply of cattle. There was a very limited market in Matamoros, Mexico, where top animals would bring as much as $11 per head. Even the hide and tallow trade was complicated by the fact that there was no major shipping point in the region from which products could be shipped to Europe. In 1859, Richard

King had tried to make a profit on his poorer cattle in the hide and tallow trade, but he was unsuccessful (Lea 1957).

When the Anglos became involved in ranching, they began to develop markets in other parts of the United States. Oral tradition tells of cattle drives to California as early as 1848, when the expanding population of that state created a reliable market. The most profitable way to sell cattle in the late 1850s was as breeding stock to those establishing their own ranches in the region. Healthy stock would bring from $12 to $18 a head. A few cattle from the area were sold in New Orleans, and some were shipped by boat to Illinois. Because the Civil War disrupted travel beginning in 1861, the market became limited to local demand, and cattle prices declined to $2 a head (Lea 1957).

Following the Civil War, ranchers were successful in developing a system of marketing their cattle at the packing plants in Kansas City, Chicago and St. Louis. A $5 steer in Reconstruction Texas was worth from $20 to $40 in Chicago, if a rancher could get it there. By 1866, large herds of cattle were headed up the cattle trails to the railheads in Missouri and Kansas. The growing practice of buying cattle to stock the open ranges of the Southwest and West (including the vast grasslands of Nebraska, the Dakotas, Colorado, New Mexico, Wyoming, Montana, and the Rockies), also provided an excellent market for Texas cattle. Between 1866 and 1890, more than five million head of cattle were driven from South Texas to these markets. An animal worth $2 in South Texas could be sold for $20 or more in Abilene or Dodge City, Kansas. The market was not always constant, however. In September of 1873, Black Friday struck Wall Street and the livestock market crashed, not to recover for two years. Between 1875 and 1885, on the other hand, the market boomed (Lea 1957).

Two types of cattle drives were organized in South Texas. Individual ranchers could either hire crews of cowboys to drive their cattle directly to the markets to the north or west, or they could wait for cattle buyers to come into the area and take the cattle they purchased to the various markets. Many of the Mexican-

American ranchers chose the latter method of selling their cattle.

Richard King, one of the earliest and most successful marketers of cattle in the region, shipped some 70,000 cattle between 1869 and 1885. His method was to have the trail drivers invest in and become part owners of the cattle. As they traveled toward the railheads, the trail boss would stay in contact with King via telegraph, so that King was often the person who made the final sale. In 1875, he made a net profit of $50,000 on a single herd of 4,737 cattle (Lea 1957).

Cattle drives originating in South Texas moved up either the Western Trail (to railheads in Dodge City, Kansas, and beyond), or up the Eastern or Chisholm Trail to Abilene, Kansas. From the Western Trail, cattle herds could connect with the Potter & Bacon Trail into Colorado; the Jim Stinson Trail into New Mexico, Arizona, and California; or the Goodnight/Loving Trail through Colorado into Wyoming. Herds of cattle numbering from one thousand to four thousand head were gathered in late February or March, when the grass in South Texas started to grow. They would follow the growth of new spring grass and arrive at their northern destinations in late summer (Dary 1981).

A "road herd" of three thousand cattle required a herd or trail boss, around ten cowboys, a cook (who was also in charge of the team and the wagon carrying supplies and bedrolls), and a wrangler (who tended the *remuda,* or string of extra horses—about six for each cowboy). About a third of the trail drivers were Mexican-American *vaqueros* or black cowboys. The trail boss would normally ride ahead of the herd, followed by the chuck wagon, which was pulled by mules or oxen. To one side of the cattle, the horse wrangler herded the remuda. Point riders had the job of guiding the lead steers. Swing riders kept the herd together, as did the flank riders a little farther back. Behind the herd, making sure that no cattle dropped out, rode the drag riders, most often the youngest cowboys with the least experience. They "ate dust" in dry weather, but kept the cattle moving. By mid-afternoon the cook, accompanied by the horse wrangler and his *remuda,* would drive the chuck wagon ahead to the night's campsite, identified by the trail boss. Although they lasted less than two decades, these trail drives and the cowboys who participated in them captured the imagination of the nation, spread the ranching culture throughout the greater Southwest, and initiated the cowboy as perhaps America's most important mythic folk hero, despite the reality of his harsh, poorly paid, insecure job (Dary 1981).

A number of important factors led to the decline of the trail drive era. Most important was the three-year drought which began in 1881, causing water sources to dry up and decreasing the amount of grass normally available. This made it much more difficult to drive cattle over such great distances. The cattle market in South Texas was also affected by growing competition from ranchers in other parts of the West and Southwest. Texas Fever, a fatal cattle disease transmitted through ticks, was another factor leading to the decline of the trail drive. Northern ranchers, afraid the disease would be spread to their cattle, organized "Winchester Quarantines," armed bands of men who gathered on the trails to keep Texas cattle out. This problem would not be solved until just before the turn of the century. Another important factor was the decline, by the mid-1880s, in the open range. In many areas, barbed-wire fences were built across the cattle trails and guarded by the farmers and ranchers who had settled there (Dary 1981).

A final nail in the coffin of the trail drive was the coming of the railroad. In 1881, the Texas Mexican Railway connected Laredo and other smaller communities to Corpus Christi, which already had rail contact with San Antonio and the rest of the nation (Lea 1957). Shortly afterward, ranchers from throughout the region began to ship their cattle by rail to northern markets. Until well into the next century, however, shorter cattle drives were still necessary to transfer cattle from the many ranches in the region to the shipping points along the railroad. The Armstrong Ranch, for instance, conducted seventy-five-mile cattle drives for many years to get cattle to its shipping point (Smith 1986). Although most ranches were soon enclosed with barbed wire fences, ranchers co-operated with one another to make sure that everyone had access to the shipping stations.

The End of the Open Range

Perhaps the most important impact Anglo thinking and technology had on the 800-year-old institution called the ranch was the end of open range ranching. This profound change can be traced to the decision Kenedy and King made in 1868 to divide up their lands (Lea 1957). Both men had a strong belief that one didn't really own the land unless he had control over it. They also felt that livestock breeding programs would be difficult, if not impossible, until the land was enclosed with fencing. Furthermore, they reasoned that fences would help protect their land and cattle from trespassers, thieves, and squatters.

Fencing was extremely time consuming and expensive until barbed wire became available in 1874. Most ranches had corrals of various sizes made of mesquite—the *corrales de leña* adopted from the Spanish and Mexican ranchers. Kenedy and King, however, went to Louisiana and made large purchases of creosoted cypress posts and pine planks, twenty feet long, one-and-a-half inches thick, and six inches wide. These were shipped by boat to Corpus Christi and hauled to the ranch on wagons. Before the fence was completed, Kenedy announced in the Corpus Christi newspaper that if anyone had cattle on Kenedy land, he had better remove them. As Lea has noted:

By completing thirty miles of heavy post and three-plank fencing across the throat of the peninsula [two sides of the ranch were bounded by the Laguna Madre] which formed the Laureles grant, Kenedy effectively enclosed the 131,000 acres of his new purchase and became the owner of the first fenced range of any real size west of the Mississippi. (1957)

Since King's land was not bounded on two sides by water, fencing the Santa Gertrudis Ranch was significantly more expensive. By the end of 1868, he had built a fence around the ranch headquarters, but it was a couple of years later before his ranch was enclosed. Other ranchers quickly followed the example of King and Kenedy, and by 1883, most of the ranches in the region were enclosed by fences, bringing to an end forever the system of open-range livestock raising which had originated in Spain in the eleventh century (Lea 1957).

Another important technology introduced into cattle ranching in the 1870s was the windmill. As early as the 1850s, King and others had used the mule-drawn *fresno* to build earthen dams, a technology which was a significant improvement over the Spanish and Mexican *mecapal* and *guaripa* (Lea 1957). But the results were the same—a reservoir of water to meet the needs of large herds of cattle. Until around the turn of the century, all wells in South Texas were dug by hand, a practice which placed significant limitations on the depth of these wells. Set over the same hand-dug wells, windmills provided a large supply of water with far less manpower required.

Vaquero *Equipment*

While the basic equipment of the South Texas *vaquero* was well established before the coming of the Anglos into South Texas, some changes began to occur. Many of the earlier *vaqueros* made their own equipment—including saddles—on Mexican *haciendas*, a practice brought to South Texas. In 1865, the King Ranch began a saddle shop to make saddles for its own *vaqueros* and others in the region who wanted to buy them. One of the popular styles of this period was the Mother Hubbard, which had leather covers over the basic saddle (Beattie 1961). Boots and various kinds of clothes—hats, pants, shirts, bandannas, etc.—were available through the ranch stores or other area stores. Blacksmiths on some of the ranches made bridle bits and spurs.

Many *vaqueros* continued to make their own equipment, particularly those artifacts of rawhide and horsehair. Rawhide lariats were commonly made on the ranches, as they had been for centuries on *haciendas* in Mexico. They also made *chicotes* (cattle whips), quirts, bridle reins, hackamores, *bosales* (nose-pieces for bridles or hackamores), and *mecates* (short ropes, called

The wife of the *vaquero* and laborer made clothes, cooked, tended gardens, cared for the house, nurtured and nursed the children, and like the *dueña,* often had her own home altar, where she worshipped and where she taught her children to worship. Courtesy Russell Lee Collection, The Center for American History, The University of Texas at Austin.

Top: Water tank made of *sillares* (caliche blocks) on the Armstrong Ranch in Jim Hogg County. Built in the 1880s, it is still in use, although two watering troughs have recently been added to the sides. Courtesy Joe S. Graham.

Right: This *noria con buque* (well with bucket) is located on the Armstrong Ranch near Hebbronville, in Jim Hogg County. Built in the 1880s, it has recently dried up due to a drop in the sub-surface water table. Courtesy Joe S. Graham.

Left: Windmill over a hand-dug well, as was the procedure when windmills first arrived in South Texas about 1880. Courtesy Joe S. Graham.

Below: Original *sillar* ranch house at Mota de Olmos, Duval County, built in the early 1850s. When Indians were in the area, the family gathered food and water, secured the doors, and climbed to the flat *chipichil* roof. Courtesy Ruben Escobar Family.

One of two similar houses built on the El Guajillo Ranch in Duval County in the early 1860s by Antonio Hinojosa. Unlike most Tejano houses of the times, these had a pitched roof made of machine-cut lumber and factory-made wooden shingles hauled from Corpus Christi on wagons. Courtesy Joe S. Graham.

Early corrals on the Norias Division of the King Ranch made of cut lumber. In the 1870s, these began to replace *corrales de leña* on Anglo ranches in South Texas. Photo taken in 1913. Courtesy King Ranch Archives.

Offside view of Texas saddle. Courtesy U.S. Army Field Artillery and Fort Sill Museum.

Offside view of Hope saddle. Courtesy U. S. Army Field Artillery and Fort Sill Museum.

McCartys by Anglos) of braided rawhide. Horsehair equipment they made included *cabrestos,* bridle reins, headstalls, cinches for saddles, and other objects, such as belts. Some wove saddle blankets from wool. Many also continued to make their own *chappareras,* although the leather workers in the King Ranch saddle shop also made and sold these (Graham 1991b).

Architecture

Mexican Americans in South Texas continued to build in the traditional style of earlier periods even though exposed to new styles of architecture brought by the Anglos. The *casas mayores* continued to be built of *sillares,* and the *peón* class continued to live in *jacales.* The main ranch house built in the 1850s by the Bazán family on the Mota de Olmos Ranch, for instance, consisted of a large room made of *sillares.* When threatened by Indians, the family gathered food and water, secured the doors from inside, and climbed onto the roof through an opening. Parapets, with *troneras* through which Bazán and his men could fire, extended about five feet above the *chipichil* roof (Graham 1992).

Antonio Hinojosa settled the El Guajillo Ranch in southern Duval County in the early 1860s. The two main houses of the original ranch headquarters were made of *sillar* blocks, but unlike most houses of this period built by Tejanos, these two had pitched roofs made of cut lumber and wooden shingles hauled from Corpus Christi on wagons. Other structures also had unique characteristics. The fortress-like home on the López ranch in Jim Hogg County is a two-story *sillar* building with a round tower (*torreón*) connected to it by a ten-foot high wall (Graham 1992).

Anglos brought their own architecture into the region, and their example influenced some of the Mexican-American builders. The walls of the main house on the Las Albercas Ranch house (in Webb County near Mirando City) are made of *sillares* quarried from a nearby hill, but the architecture is significantly different from other Mexican-made buildings of this era. Workers on this ranch also lived in a bunkhouse rather than in *jacales.*

Perhaps the first bunkhouse in the area was built on the King Ranch for its single *vaqueros* and workers (Lea 1957). Richard King married Henrietta Chamberlain in 1854, and the first house they lived in was, in Henrietta's words, "a mere *jacal*" (Lea 1957). The house King built for his family was described as follows:

. . . low and rambling, built of frame, with an attic or half second-story and an inviting, bannistered front gallery. The dining room and kitchen, built of stone to avoid the hazard of fire, formed a separate building at the rear and was connected with the living quarters by an unroofed walkway open to the weather. A little to the north of this main house was the stone-built commissary and store, together with a kitchen, eating space and sleeping quarters for extra hands, teamsters and those who came seeking work at the ranch. By the commissary stood a watchtower, and a men's dormitory for buyers, visitors and chance travelers. Farther to the north were stables, corrals, carriage and wagon sheds, a busy blacksmith's shop and a rough line of small houses where ranch employees lived with their families. Sometime in the 1860s a one-room school was established for children on the ranch, doubtless under supervision by Henrietta King. (Lea 1957)

Much of the lumber used to build these structures was secondhand material bought from the government when the Army post and depot in Corpus Christi was abandoned in 1857. Other lumber came from Louisiana and Florida, brought through Corpus Christi and hauled to the ranch by oxcart and heavy wagon.

The Ranch Modernizes: 1885–1930

By 1885, the open range was a thing of the past in South Texas. Much ranchland would become farmland, particularly along the Lower Rio Grande Valley, locally called "The Valley." New towns began to spring up as more people migrated into South Texas from Mexico and various parts of the United States. Deep wells and windmills played a major role in the modernization of the ranch, leading to the crossfencing of the land and bringing such advances as the upbreeding of cattle and the eradication of the tick which caused Texas Fever.

Changes in the Wind: Drilling Rigs and the Windmills

Perhaps the greatest boon to the South Texas ranching industry after the end of open range was the successful quest for adequate supplies of potable water for the growing number of livestock in the region. Prior to the turn of the century, watering places were so few and far between that only about ten percent of the land was close enough to an adequate water supply to be used for cattle. As Richard King complained, "Where I have grass, I have no water. And where I have water, I have no grass." In 1889 many cattle on the King Ranch were dying from drinking bad water, and by the time of the drought of 1891 the ranch had to ship 12,000 cattle to Indian Territory to save their lives. The next year, with the help of the Army, the King Ranch initiated a series of rainmaking efforts—noisy discharges of explosives directed skyward—which proved unsuccessful (Lea 1957).

The numerous hand-dug wells on ranches all over South Texas were shallow (a hundred or so feet deep), and sometimes the water was not potable. Many areas had no wells at all because the water table was too deep to reach digging by hand. The King Ranch made a significant contribution to solving this problem throughout the region. In 1898, the ranch's Robert Kleberg put up the money to buy heavy drilling equipment from the Dempster Mill Manufacturing Corporation of Beatrice, Nebraska. On June 6 the following year, at a depth of 532 feet, the drill hit water, resulting in an artesian well which produced about seventy-five gallons of pure, clear water per minute. By the end of 1900, there were twenty-two producing wells on the ranch, and by 1907, there were sixty-seven, ranging in depth from 402 feet to 704 feet. In many cases, windmills were necessary to bring the water to the surface. It was then stored in earthen tanks. Eventually the ranch built concrete watering troughs about thirty feet across and three feet deep, buried in the ground two feet. By the mid-1950s, the ranch had 381 water wells: 101 were artesian, 14 had power pumps to produce water, and 266 used windmills. Each of the four divisions of the ranch had a full-time windmill crew, with about twenty-five men working to take care of this valuable resource (Lea 1957).

Other ranches in the region followed suit. For example, by 1903, the Armstrong Ranch had twenty-one artesian wells providing water for its livestock (Smith 1986). This new source of water was important for ranchers because it increased the efficiency of land use from about twenty percent to over eighty percent.

The earliest windmills in South Texas, made by Eclipse, had wooden blades and wooden towers, but by the 1930s the majority were made by Aeromotor and had metal blades and towers (Baker 1992). While the large ranches hired fulltime maintenance men for their windmills, many a cowboy on the smaller ranches found himself assigned the new task of maintaining windmills.

Cattle Breeds: From the Longhorn to the Santa Gertrudis

New technologies and smaller pastures led to up-breeding of cattle and even the creation of the first new breed developed in the United States, the Santa Gertrudis. Longhorns, which prospered on the open range, were gradually replaced by such breeds as Brahmans, Herefords, Shorthorns, and various crossbreeds. As early as the 1870s, Anglo ranchers had tried to improve the quality of their cattle by introducing Durham bulls and other breeds, but they had little success before the open range was finally crossfenced. Robert Kleberg brought bulls to the King Ranch from East Texas, Kansas, Mississippi, Illinois and even Canada to breed with Longhorn cows. In 1886, he introduced Shorthorn and Hereford bulls onto the ranch, breeding a purebred Shorthorn to 100 cows isolated in one pasture. In 1910, he introduced the first Brahman blood on the ranch via a huge, black half-breed Brahman/Shorthorn bull (Lea 1957).

In 1920, a calf named Monkey, destined to become a famous sire, was born on the King Ranch. He was an active sire until 1932, producing some 150 productive male offspring. Monkey was the foundation sire of the Santa Gertrudis breed, the first distinctive breed of

American cattle, recognized officially by the USDA in 1940 (Lea 1957). Lea makes an interesting point about the development of the Santa Gertrudis breed:

The first distinctive American breed of cattle was created not by trained geneticists equipped with a research laboratory and a scientific experimental station, but by a family of practicing ranchers using their own judgement, their own livestock, their own pastures, and their own money to shape what they themselves needed for the profitable pursuit of their own business. (1957)

The King Ranch also played a part in the eradication of Texas Fever, (also called Tick Fever), which had led to the quarantine of Texas cattle in northern markets in the 1870s and 1880s. After consultation with scientists from the Bureau of Animal Industries, Richard Kleberg invented, built, and put into use at the ranch in 1891 the world's first cattle dipping vat. The ticks were eradicated from the land by keeping the host cattle from it for a year. In 1928, the USDA declared South Texas to be free of the ticks which caused Tick Fever, which had plagued the South Texas cattle industry for some sixty years (Lea 1957).

Modern Transportation Reaches South Texas

The railroad had officially arrived in South Texas in 1881, when the Texas Mexican Railway connected Laredo and Corpus Christi. The year 1888 saw the San Antonio and Aransas Pass Railroad connect Corpus Christi to San Antonio, linking South Texas ranches to markets throughout the U.S. and bringing new technologies and materials into the region. Shipping points were established at various locations along the tracks, from which ranchers could ship their cattle. The Collins station, for instance—about twenty miles northwest of the headquarters of the King Ranch— also served the Armstrong Ranch located seventy-five miles from there. Unfortunately, many South Texas ranches were still too far from railroad shipping stations to be able to take advantage of the new technology (Lea 1957).

In 1904, as a result of the efforts of many ranchers and businessmen in South Texas, the St. Louis,

Brownsville, and Mexico Railway connected Corpus Christi to Brownsville. There were twenty-one stations established between Robstown and Brownsville, some of which would become thriving towns. A shipping point at the Norias station, used by many in deep South Texas, was the place where the King Ranch, in 1913, built the largest set of shipping pens in the region (Lea 1957).

By 1930, railroads and roads connected most ranches and farms to towns, thereby decreasing isolation. Cars, pickups, and large cattle trucks replaced wagons and stagecoaches, as roads—both paved and unpaved— began linking communities. As a result, the once tightly-knit ranching communities became smaller as families moved into nearby towns. Cattle drives continued in some areas until the 1940s. The last one on the Jones Ranch, for instance, was a forty-two-mile drive from southern Jim Hogg County to Hebbronville just prior to WW II (W. W. Jones interview).

The car and the pickup brought a new mobility to South Texas ranch people. In 1850, a round trip by ox-cart from Zapata to Laredo (about fifty-three miles), took eight days in good weather (Lott and Martínez 1953). By 1930, the trip by car took only eight hours, even on the rough, unpaved roads. At present, one can make the trip in two hours. Ranches that were once self-sufficient became more and more dependent on supplies bought from stores in nearby towns.

Changes for the Cowboy

The coming of barbed wire and the windmill to South Texas meant that cowboys no longer participated in multi-ranch roundups twice a year or long cattle drives to northern markets. Also, as pastures became smaller, fewer horsemen were necessary. Another change in cowboy life came around 1890, when the cause of Texas Fever was confirmed. Cowboys learned to use dipping vats to help kill the ticks that caused the disease, and to leave selected pastures empty each year to allow ticks without a "host" to die. One can still find abandoned cement dipping vats on many ranches in the region, surrounded by corrals in disrepair.

Many of the cattle-working methods of earlier days,

however, remained essentially the same even though practiced on a smaller scale. Cattle were rounded up in individual pastures and roped, tied, branded, and marked in corrals made of creosoted posts and heavy planks, a system which had its advantages. For one thing, it required fewer cowboys, and for another, it did not make the cattle wild like chasing them through brush did.

Mexican-American *vaqueros* continued to outnumber Anglo cowboys on South Texas ranches, which is the case even today. Many ranchers preferred the *vaquero,* who tended to be married, stable, and often worked for one ranch for a long period of time. Anglo cowboys, often bachelors who moved frequently from place to place, had been more important during the era of cattle drives (Montejano 1987).

Vaqueros and cowboys continued working mostly with cattle, especially during branding and marking time, but those on smaller ranches also began to spend time caring for windmills, as well as building and repairing watering troughs and miles of barbed-wire fences.

During the drought of 1916–1918, when the annual rainfall in South Texas was less than eight inches per year, it became necessary on some ranches to feed the cattle daily, mostly with cottonseed cake. The prickly pear cactus growing in the region became an important source of cattle feed, but the thorns had to be removed first. One man, with a kerosene torch made especially for this purpose, could burn enough prickly pear each day to feed about a hundred cattle. The larger ranchers employed crews of these "pear burners," while smaller ranchers relied on their *vaqueros* (Lea 1957).

New Materials, New Architecture

New means of transportation made available new building materials which influenced the ranch architecture of South Texas. Cut lumber, cement, kiln-fired bricks, factory-made doors and windows, and metal roofing began to replace the local building materials. Hardware and fasteners—latches, hinges, screening, nails and screws—replaced the handmade fixtures.

For the working-class, the *jacal* was slowly replaced by the small board-and-batten house (*casa de madera parada*) made of cut lumber shipped by rail into Corpus Christi, Laredo, and Brownsville. Not everyone could afford these structures, however, and many continued to live in *jacales,* particularly on the smaller ranches along the Rio Grande.

Larger ranches began providing houses of lumber for their *vaqueros* and workers. The King Ranch and Kenedy's La Parra Ranch, for example, began building houses of lumber as soon as it become readily available. On the La Parra Ranch, the families of *vaqueros* and other workers were provided with small, one-room, board-and-batten dwellings of approximately the same size as the earlier *jacales.* Often, two families lived in the same structure, which consisted of two rooms divided by a solid wall (Villarreal 1972).

New buildings would combine both the old and new styles. Houses were often built one room wide and several rooms long, with doors and windows placed to take advantage of any breeze which might pass through and cool the house. In the fall of 1886, John Armstrong and Don Fermín completed the new ranch headquarters for the Armstrong family. Made of wood, it consisted of a main house, a dining room and kitchen together, two small cottages, and a group of *jacales.* All had thatched roofs of *sacahuiste* grass tied with yucca fibers. Another new home for the family was built in 1892. Called the "Chicago Ranch," it had wide porches front and back, and extensions at each end extending back to form a patio enclosed on three sides. Each room had an enclosed bathroom. Water for the house was pumped into a tank by windmill (Smith 1986). W. W. Jones's father, A. C. Jones, in 1904 built the main house on the Alta Vista Ranch, using a board-and-batten structure with a wide porch along the end. The back and roof were made of wooden shingles.

In 1912, the main house on the King Ranch, built in the 1850s, burned down. Interestingly, the model for the new main house was an impressive *casa grande* from a *hacienda* in Mexico which Robert Kleberg had seen in one of his visits there. It required two years and

$350,000 to build and consisted of twenty-five rooms, each with its own fireplace, with many bathrooms and wide, cool verandas. It was finished in 1915 (Lea 1957).

Social Organization of a South Texas Ranch

Changes in the old *patrón* system took place only slowly. Some ranches in South Texas remained very traditional. Mifflin Kenedy's 375,000-acre La Parra Ranch in Kenedy County maintained the old two-level social order of the earlier *haciendas* well into the 1960s (Villarreal 1970).

The La Parra Ranch was composed of two divisions, the Mifflin Kenedy Division and the Laurel Leaf Division. Each division had a *corrida* or cow camp; a *campo de apie* crew which worked "afoot" building fence, clearing brush, and repairing fences and corrals; and a series of *ranchitos*, two- and three-man stations assigned to look after livestock. A windmill crew took care of all of the windmills on the ranch. The *corridas* had ten to thirty *vaqueros*, a *remudero* or horse wrangler, and a *cocinero* or camp cook, all supervised by a *caporal* assisted by a *caudillo*. The *campos* were made up of about twenty laborers supervised by a *mayordomo*, who was assisted by a *segundo*. The early *caporales* were Anglos, but since shortly after 1900, most have been Mexican Americans (Villarreal 1970).

Into the early 1960s, Kenedy *vaqueros* lived in cow camps and spent their time working cattle or breaking horses. In addition to being fine riders, *vaqueros* had to be skilled at driving or herding cattle, cutting cattle from the herd, and roping. Many took pride in their work and their skills, and some became well-known performers. As one *vaquero* noted, the life of a *vaquero* was "interesting" and at times almost "romantic," but would "never make a man rich" (Villarreal 1970).

Male children on the ranch were expected to begin working for the ranch at about eight years of age. They started as yard cleaners, and by the time they were ten, they would begin working in *corridas* or *campos*. Villarreal (1970) notes that the loyalty of earlier Mexican *vaqueros* can be seen in the case of Encarnación Morales, whose five sons, a step-son, and two sons-in-law began working on the Kenedy ranch in 1882. As of the 1970s, five generations of the Morales family had worked on the ranch: twenty-five grandsons, two grandsons-in-law, fifteen great-grandsons, and seven great-great-grandsons.

Vaquero *Equipment*

Certain *vaquero* equipment remained basically the same, including the quirt, the *chicote* (cattle whip), spurs, the bridle, bridle reins, and saddle blankets. *Vaqueros* continued to impress outsiders with their skills with this equipment. For example, Maude Gilliland recalls in her memoirs that in the summer of 1902 her family traveled in wagons from Corpus Christi to Rancho Capisallo, located in Cameron and Hidalgo Counties, to be with their father, who was the ranch manager. Accompanied by two Tejano *vaqueros* on horseback, the family witnessed some remarkable demonstrations of their skills:

There were thousands of wild geese on the coast in those days and we weren't on the road long before we saw a large flock. The Mexicans killed several. These men were experts in the art of popping their long plaited raw-hide whips. Just as the geese started to fly, one of the men put spurs to his horse and ran among them and with a crack like a pistol shot brought one down with his bullwhip! Mama cooked them in the big Dutch oven. (1964)

The *vaqueros* on many ranches also became proficient with new (and less romantic) equipment, like the claw-hammer and fencing pliers. The hemp lariat replaced the rawhide one not only because of hemp's greater strength and flexibility, but because of its greater availability in local feed and hardware stores. Of course, the saddle styles also changed. Although its basic shape remained similar to the modern stock saddle which had evolved by 1870, modifications continued. Some types became famous, like the Vela saddles of Floresville and saddles of the King Ranch's Running W Saddle Shop, made since 1865.

Top: The *jacal* was gradually replaced by small homes made of cut lumber. This half *jacal*/half board-and-batten structure is from the 1890s/1920s. Courtesy John E. Conner Museum.

Bottom: Beginning in the 1890s, the simple board-and-batten houses gradually replaced the *jacales* of the working class. Courtesy Joe S. Graham.

This artesian well on the King Ranch, drilled in 1903,

produced several thousand gallons of water per day. Courtesy

King Ranch Archives.

Top: Watering system on Alta Vista Ranch: tanks, troughs, and windmill. Courtesy Joe S. Graham.

Bottom: Between 1905 and 1910, on the first and third Tuesday of each month, special excursion trains took prospective Anglo homeseekers and farmers to explore the "Magic Valley" and other irrigable areas of South Texas. Courtesy Hidalgo County Historical Museum.

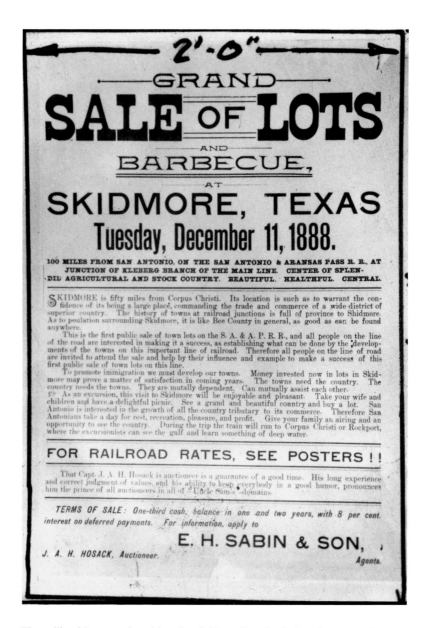

Flyers like this one, advertising South Texas farm lands for sale, attracted

farmers from the Midwest. Courtesy John E. Conner Museum.

Top left: Anglos brought in the mule-drawn *fresno* to build earthen dams, an important technological innovation in the region. They were used on ranches as well as in the oil fields. Courtesy The Dr. Fred'k McGregor Photo Collection of the Corpus Christi Museum.

Above: Early irrigation canal and system under construction, about 1915. Irrigation canals made possible a boom in cultivated lands along the Rio Grande. Courtesy Hidalgo County Historical Museum.

Top right: Two early automobiles on the Alta Vista Ranch in southern Jim Hogg County. The car and the pickup brought a new mobility to South Texas ranch people. Photo taken around 1925. Courtesy W. W. Jones Family Archives.

Top: Modern ranching methods led to a decline in the number of cowboys required to care for the cattle, but ranchers also needed field hands to raise hay and other feed crops for their livestock. Courtesy Hidalgo County Historical Museum.

Bottom: A new type of labor force was created in South Texas—migrant labor—which followed the crops from the lower Rio Grande Valley northward toward the Neuces River and eventually into other states. Courtesy Hidalgo County Historical Museum.

Top: Mexican laborers transformed mesquite-covered pastureland into tillable farmland with the grubbing hoe. Courtesy Hidalgo County Historical Museum.

Bottom: The loyalty of earlier Mexican *vaqueros* can be seen in the case of Encarnación Morales, whose five sons, a stepson, and two sons-in-law began working on the Kenedy ranch in 1882. Courtesy Roberto Villarreal.

Top: The *presa* (dam) at El Randado, built in the 1830s. After 150 years, the reservoir is still used to water cattle. Courtesy Joe S. Graham.

Left: An early handmade cement watering trough. Courtesy Joe S. Graham.

Right: An old dipping vat on El Cameron Ranch in Zapata County, built in the 1930s, used to kill ticks that caused "Texas Fever." It hasn't been used in decades. Courtesy Joe S. Graham.

Below: Feed trough on the Armstrong Ranch in Jim Hogg County, where cowboys put feed for cattle. Courtesy Joe S. Graham.

A typical roundup on a South Texas ranch, about 1920.

Courtesy King Ranch Archives.

Right: Oil rig blowout west of Corpus Christi, 8 November 1922. On ranches enjoying the oil boom, cattle raising often became secondary. Courtesy The Dr. Fred'k McGregor Photo Collection of the Corpus Christi Museum.

Below: Drilling for oil in South Texas in the early 1920s. Courtesy The Dr. Fred'k McGregor Photo Collection of the Corpus Christi Museum.

Top: Deserted oil tanks from the 1920s and 1930s can still be found on many ranches. Courtesy Joe S. Graham.

Bottom: Ranch entranceway built of castaway oil field pipe and drill stem at Bustamante's in Zapata County. Courtesy Joe S. Graham.

The Fight Against Brush

In the early 1890s, larger ranches like the King Ranch, which could afford to hire large numbers of workers, made a concerted effort to fight the growing problem of encroaching brushlands (Lea 1957). Early ranchers remembered a time when the wide, open plains held tall, thick grass, with the few brush thickets found primarily along the Rio Grande and a few arroyos in the region. As a consequence of overgrazing and of the fact that the cattle spread the thorny bushes (particularly mesquite) wherever they went, these brush thickets became a serious problem which continues today.

In early 1900, the King Ranch employed a strategy which would prove most useful in the Lower Rio Grande Valley. They hired transient Mexican laborers to chop brush and grub roots with axes, picks, and grubbing hoes. The ranch paid five dollars for each acre cleaned, fifty cents for every cord of firewood cut, and varying prices for cut posts which could be used in fences or corrals. The ranch also provided weekly rations to its workers: seven pounds of flour, one pound of coffee, two pounds of beans, one pound of rice, a pound and a half of bacon, and one quart of molasses. By 1915, the ranch had cleared about 17,000 acres, mostly in its headquarters area (Lea 1957).

Around the turn of the century, large numbers of midwestern farmers began moving to The Valley to farm, rather than to ranch. One reason was that farming produced more income per acre than did cattle raising. Some ranches needed about fifteen to twenty acres per animal, clearly not an economical use of the land compared to a farming operation. Additional problems challenged ranchers but did not affect farmers. Following World War I, the nation suffered a serious decline in the cattle market, reaching its bottom in 1925. In that year, about ninety-five percent of western cattle loan companies went into liquidation and thousands of stockmen lost their ranches (Lea 1957).

Irrigation and Farming in South Texas: Impact on Ranching

Beginning in the early 1900s, the discovery of artesian wells, new irrigation techniques, dry land farming, and better railroad service brought about an increase in cultivated lands—particularly in the Lower Rio Grande Valley, where mesquite jungles were being transformed into plowed fields. Between 1905 and 1910, on the first and third Tuesdays of each month, special excursion trains took prospective Anglo homeseekers and farmers to explore the "Magic Valley" and other irrigable areas of South Texas. These settlers bought land, settled into communities planned by ranchers or land developers, planted profitable cash crops, and sought out Mexican day laborers (Lea 1957 and Montejano 1987).

Land which sold for $4 an acre in 1905 sold for $22 an acre in 1910, the year in which the first bale of cotton was harvested at Mercedes, Texas; the first oranges and grapefruit were picked in the region in commercial quantities; and the U.S. dollar replaced the Mexican *peso* as the currency in general circulation there. In 1907, the three-year-old railroad between Brownsville and Corpus Christi hauled about 500 carloads of farm products from the Lower Rio Grande Valley, and by 1925, that number increased to 35,362 rail cars (Lea 1957). In short, between 1900 and 1930, South Texas experienced an agricultural revolution.

Between 1910 and 1930, farms in Cameron County quadrupled in number, from 709 to 2936; in Hidalgo County farms grew five-fold in number, from 677 to 4327. Populations in Cameron, Hidalgo, Willacy, and Nueces Counties doubled between 1900 and 1920 (from 79,934 to 159,842) and again by 1930, to 322,845. On the other hand, the number of cattle in Starr, Hidalgo, and Cameron Counties fell by almost fifty percent between 1910 and 1920, a drop from 174,513 head to 99,597 head (Montejano 1987).

Along the Rio Grande, towns once sustained by ranching became farming communities, and new towns such as Bishop, Driscoll, Robstown, and Raymondville sprang up in South Texas, particularly along the railroad. The discovery of artesian wells had sparked a great interest in farming in the arid lands in Nueces County. In 1919, Mrs. Henrietta King sold 34,833 acres of land (for $22.50 per acre) to P. A. Chapman, a wealthy oil man from Waxahachie. He bought another 6000 acres the same year. The "Chapman Ranch" farming operation, located some sixteen miles south of Corpus Christi, was looked upon as a model farming development for the area (Lea 1957).

Modern ranching methods had led to a decline in the number of cowboys required to care for the cattle, but farming still required manual labor. A new type of labor force was created in South Texas—migrant labor—families who followed the crops from the lower Rio Grande Valley northward toward the Nueces River and eventually into other states. Although many of these were Mexican field laborers, some were cowboys whose services were no longer needed on ranches.

From Ranch to Agribusiness: 1930–Present

Changes in South Texas ranching came about from new technologies that were part of major economic, social, and political changes. The most dramatic—the end of open range, the drilling of deep water wells and the windmill—came after some 800 years of ranching which had maintained a fairly stable and traditional way of life. After 1930, new technologies created more rapid changes in ranch life.

The challenges faced by modern ranchers are neatly summarized in a recent study, whose authors state:

South Texas traditionally has been known as home to some of the most prominent ranches in history. However, as elsewhere, the economic climate of the past fifteen years has led to changes in the general profitability picture for South Texas Ranchers. Increased competition, increased costs, application of new technologies and optimum management of available resources make producing beef profitably an increasingly difficult and complex task. This is compounded by the diverse and variable weather patterns of South Texas. Ranchers are continually searching for new ways to become more competitive and profitable. (Carson, Paschal, and Hanselka, 1992)

Income from the oil boom in the 1920s and 1930s, social changes during World War II, and the regional increase in paved roads and vehicles, combined with enhanced technology, completed the transformation of the old Spanish *hacienda*-type ranch into a modern, profit-oriented, diversified business. To maximize profits, ranch managers pressed aggressively to reduce labor costs and experiment with new capital ventures, including planting crops on their land and leasing it for hunting purposes.

Ranches have been greatly reduced in size and number in some counties in South Texas as a consequence of modern technology making it more profitable to farm the land. For example, Nueces County, which a century before was all ranch land, has only two ranches operating in its boundaries in the 1990s. Likewise, in Duval County, which was all ranch land a century ago, there are about 200,000 acres under cultivation, out of a total land area of 1,089,920 acres (over 18 percent of the total land). On the other hand, some counties have remained primarily ranch land. In 1990, for example, Jim Hogg County, which has a total of 729,600 acres, has only about seven percent of its land under cultivation, with most of the rest owned by ranchers (USDA offices in Corpus Christi, Texas).

Finding Oil and Gas: Ranchers Get a Break

The oil boom which began in South Texas in the 1920s and 1930s, along with the gas boom of the 1970s and 1980s, helped many marginal ranches survive, and even modernize and expand their operations. Fortunes were made by both descendants of original ranching families and newcomers to the area. New communities grew out of the oil boom, diversifying the region's economy with new jobs and businesses.

The oil industry began in East Texas in 1901 with the discovery at Spindletop. Even though oil was not discovered in South Texas until 1913, oil companies began leasing the area's lands that same year, leading to many new lawsuits over land ownership and the precise location of boundaries. Even the government of the State of Texas began instituting a number of lawsuits and pursuing titles to its public lands, particularly those connected to Spanish and Mexican land grants. Many ranchers who had long thought their titles secure discovered they had to renew their fight—this time in the courts. The net result was a clearing of titles and more careful surveying of the land (Lea 1957).

The King Ranch provides an interesting example of what happened on many South Texas ranches. In 1901, the ranch leased acreage for oil exploration and drilling to A. J. Vick, but the lease was canceled in 1902. Five years later eastern capitalists and land developers offered Mrs. King $10 million for the ranch, which she refused (Lea 1957). In the early 1920s, Humble Oil and Refining Company leased King Ranch land and explored for oil, discovering some indications of its presence but drilling no productive wells. They allowed the lease to lapse, then leased it again in 1933, along with many other South Texas properties. At that point, Humble paid a bonus of thirteen cents an acre and promised one barrel of oil to the landowner for every eight it pumped. Oil was finally discovered on the ranch in 1939, on the San Antonio Viejo property, and the first producing well drilled on the Santa Gertrudis division of the ranch came in 1941. This was followed by the discovery of a rich oil field on the El Sauz Ranch in 1944, and since 1945, four other minor oil locations have been discovered on the King Ranch. By 1952, the famous ranch had 650 producing oil and gas wells. By 1953, oil and gas royalties produced as much income as livestock on the ranch (Lea 1957). Although many areas in South Texas have yielded neither oil nor gas, stories similar to the King Ranch's could be told for other ranching enterprises in the region. For many of these, cattleraising often became of secondary importance.

After the oil boom slowed and ended in many parts of the region, used equipment—large oil tanks and pipe and drill stems—remained on the ranches. These have been used by ranchers in a number of ways, including using them to make corrals, cattle guards, and distinctive gate entranceways.

Pickup Trucks, Automobiles, and Trucks

In addition to the great profits, oil and gas production brought other important changes to ranching in South Texas. Tom Lea claims that the oil field roads built on the King Ranch, for instance, marked the end of an era by providing good all-weather roads connecting the various parts of the ranch. While the four-wheel-drive pickup had been introduced shortly after WW I, the pickup truck and trailer were only able to transform ranch work with the help of these roads. Says Lea:

The old horseback isolation of the work camps, the slow cattle drives from remote corners of the ranch, were relegated to the past. Time and distance shrank. Following the oil roads, combustion engines and motor vehicles became ranching implements as basic as cow horses. (1957)

On today's ranch, heavy cattle trailers can move cattle quickly from one pasture to another or even to an auction barn, where about ninety-five percent of South Texas ranchers sell their cattle (Carson, Paschal, Hanselka 1992). Where cowboys once lived and worked in isolated, remote cow camps for weeks at a time, they now live at ranch or division headquarters or in neighboring towns, and drive to work. Even on the largest ranches, the foreman can travel from one end of the ranch to the other in a couple of hours. Motorized vehicles and good roads have made ranching operations more efficient and reduced the number of *vaqueros* and cowboys needed.

Modern Science and the Modern Ranch

Significant scientific contributions to modern ranching include the elimination of screwworms, and the development of vaccines against blackleg and other bovine diseases, as well as the development of dietary supplements. The screwworm, the larva stage of the blue-green fly *Cochltomyla hominivorax,* was a major problem on ranches until the 1960s. When animals were marked, branded, castrated, dehorned, or wounded—and for a period of time just after birth—they were in danger of infection, which could kill them. During the spring and summer, cowboys had to work nearly every day, inspecting cattle and doctoring them with a powerful medication, or "dope," which killed the screwworms. In 1935, an estimated two to three million head of livestock in Texas were infested by screwworms. In the 1960s, E. F. Knipling and R. C. Bushland discovered a process for eradicating the screwworm by dropping millions of sterilized adult male screwworm flies into infested areas. These flies mated with the females, which then laid eggs that would not hatch (Richardson 1978).

Science has also helped the ranching industry by developing vaccines and diet supplements to help make livestock raising more productive. Today, around ninety-five percent of the ranchers in South Texas vaccinate their calves to prevent such diseases as blackleg and anthrax, and "drench" them (force medicine into their stomachs) to eliminate internal parasites. Most ranchers also spray their animals to reduce such pests as flies and lice (Carson, Paschal, Hanselka 1992). Adding phosphorus to water and feed and providing other mineral supplements have proved an important means of preventing "creeps," a debilitating illness resulting from diets without adequate minerals.

Improved Grazing Pastures

Another scientific development has been new equipment designed to eliminate and control the brushlands which had begun to invade South Texas ranch lands. Dissatisfied with the grubbing hoe and ax they had used since the 1890s to try to control the spread of mesquite and other brush, they began to experiment with a number of different methods. A recent survey indicates that as many as ninety-five percent of ranchers have used some type of brush management within the last ten years. Current mechanical methods of brush and weed control include shredding, roller chopping, chaining, discing, root plowing, grubbing, and bulldozing. Brush may also be controlled by spraying herbicides from the air or ground, or by putting them directly into the soil (Carson, Paschal, and Hanselka 1992).

Again, a good example of this type of effort was that of the King Ranch, which built and experimented with various types of brush-control machinery. In 1951, the ranch developed an astonishingly effective machine— a giant funnel dozer and root plow powered by dual tractors and weighing over 110,000 pounds—which could clear about four acres of brush an hour, cutting, shredding and leaving it stacked in windrows. It also pulled a sixteen-foot blade about sixteen inches below the ground surface. The cost was about four dollars per acre, and for many years the ranch had two of these giant machines working day and night. Between 1936 and 1953, the King Ranch cabled 10,700 acres, dozed 103,998 acres, and root plowed 141,264 acres of ranch land, spending some $751,259.75 to do it. Herbicides were also tried, but generally with unsatisfactory results (Lea 1957).

Rancho El Niño Felíz, owned by Diego Gutiérrez of Laredo and located in Zapata County, has been completely root plowed and all brush cleared. In cooperation with scientists at Texas A&M University, Gutiérrez has planted various types of grasses for grazing his cattle. Over the years in the region, some seventy-five percent of the ranchers in the area have experimented with grasses from many parts of the world. Some of the most common perennial grasses include Klein grass, Buffelgrass, bluestems, Bahia, and Love grass. The cost for this runs about fifty dollars per acre. Some ranchers prefer using annual species of plants, including haygrazer, Sudan, ryegrass, turnips, sorghum, and small grains like oats, wheat, and rye. This costs about thirty dollars per acre per year (Carson, Paschal, and Hanselka 1992).

Improved Livestock

While the new Santa Gertrudis breed of cattle was recognized by the USDA in 1940, the quest for the best cattle to raise in South Texas continues. Common on area ranches are Herefords, Angus, Santa Gertrudis, Brahmans, and mixed breeds. Many ranchers use various types of crossbreeds, and some continue to raise Longhorns. For example, Frank Graham, foreman on the Alta Vista Ranch in Jim Hogg County, has a herd of over a hundred longhorns which produce from sixty to seventy calves each year (Frank Graham interview). Many ranches work closely with veterinarians to improve their livestock productivity by doing fertility tests on bulls, monitoring the conception rate of cows, and using artificial insemination with the sperm from prize bulls.

The Modern Ranch Diversifies

After the early 1900s, other sources of income in addition to oil and gas revenues became important. Today, the sale of hunting leases provides some ranches with as much or more income as does selling cattle. In addition, many ranches have increased the acreage planted in cash crops. In 1991, for example, the King Ranch harvested some 40,000 acres of cotton and built a state-of-the-art cotton gin (Bruce Cheeseman interview).

A 1984 survey by the Texas Agricultural Extension Service reported that among South Texas beef producers, only thirty-eight percent of the total income came from farming and ranching (Ladewig *et al* 1984). A more recent survey indicates that among ranches which cultivate only small acreage, the sources of income include the following: livestock, sixty-five percent; wildlife, ten percent; hay and seed production, two percent; and farm row-crops and grain, ten percent. Non-ranch income sources include oil, gas, and minerals, thirty-two percent; investments, nineteen percent; business profits (other than ranching), ten percent; and salaries (including those of the ranchers' spouses), twenty-six percent (Carson, Paschal, and Hanselka 1992).

Below is a chart of the percentages of ranch income produced by the sale of cattle, horses, and other livestock for the King Ranch and the Alta Vista Ranch in 1885, 1957, and 1991.

	King Ranch	*Alta Vista Ranch*
1885	100%	100%
1957	67%	85%
1991	27%	75%

It is evident that the King Ranch has moved into agribusiness during the last sixty years, while the Alta Vista Ranch has remained a more traditional cattle ranch. Another difference between the two ranches is that while the King Ranch has enjoyed a very productive oil and gas business over the years, the Alta Vista is located in an area with no oil or gas (Lea 1957 and W. W. Jones and Bruce Cheeseman interviews).

Hunting has long been both a sport enjoyed by ranchers and ranch hands and a cheap source of meat. But the amount of ranch land leased to outside hunters has increased dramatically, accounting for a significant income for many ranchers. A recent survey indicates that about sixty percent of ranchers in South Texas offer various types of hunting leases, at an average income of about $3 per acre. They report several types of game: deer, quail, dove, feral hog, javalina, turkey, and waterfowl (Carson, Pashcal, and Hanselka 1992). There are some ranches which stock more exotic game animals, such as Axis deer, Nilgai, and black buck antelope.

The Mariposa Ranch in Jim Hogg County is almost totally reliant on hunters for its income, using cattle principally to keep the grass and brush under control so that hunting will be good. They have about 300 bird hunters and 100 deer hunters each year. The ranch sports three hunting lodges and a number of well-equipped hunting vehicles. From October through February, the ranch managers hire a group from Oklahoma who bring a number of trained bird-hunting dogs to the ranch (Robert King interview).

Fencing and Land Control

A century after the end of the open range in South Texas, ranchers continue to crossfence their land into smaller pastures, using new products like steel fence posts, heavy net wire, and steel pipe. This benefits ranch owners in the reduction of labor costs due to smaller numbers of cowboys needed, greater control over cattle breeding, and better management of grazing to maximize the number of cattle the land is able to support.

Barbed wire continues to be used throughout the region, although other types of fencing are becoming more and more popular. Heavy net wire fencing with two strands of barbed wire at the top is very popular, in part because these fences prevent animals from passing from pasture to pasture and perhaps injuring themselves as they attempt to climb between strands of barbed wire. Another change in fencing is that with the advent of hunting as a source of revenue, many ranchers are building fences from eight to ten feet high to prevent deer from leaving the ranch. These fences are most often made of two layers of net wire mounted on steel posts, with corner posts of heavy steel pipe or wolmanized posts.

Corral styles have also passed through a number of phases in South Texas. Some ranches still use the old *corrales de leña,* while others use the "second generation" types made of heavy lumber with posts of creosoted cypress or railroad ties. Modern corrals are made of steel pipe or other materials, and most have cutting chutes for separating cattle into various categories and squeeze chutes (the most modern of which are hydraulically operated) to help control animals while they are being marked and branded. Some even have branding tables built into the chutes. Most have loading chutes or ramps which are used to load cattle onto trailers or onto large cattle trucks.

Water Continues to Be Important

Water control mechanisms continue to be improved. One can still find the old *norias con buque* on many ranches, but they are historic relics. Although some hand-dug wells are still in use, most ranches in the region employ drilling companies to dig wells and maintain the equipment used to pump water.

While windmills are still critical because of limited access to electricity, many ranchers have replaced some of them with electric pumps, which are less expensive, more reliable, and easier to maintain. Repair and maintenance of windmills are the responsibility of cowboys on many smaller ranches, but the larger ones use maintenance crews or contract with outside companies to do the work.

A variety of tanks and reservoirs are used on the modern ranch to store water. Some still rely on dirt tanks—either those built earlier with *fresnoes* pulled by mules or those built by modern heavy equipment like the bulldozer. For example, in the 1950s on Rancho El Niño Feliz, a large dam was built which resulted in a reservoir with fifteen surface acres of water, used to provide for cattle and to sell to oil and gas drilling companies working in the area (Diego Gutiérrez interview). On other ranches, old water storage tanks made of different materials are being used—some made of caliche blocks plastered with lime, others of cypress. Most of these, however, have been abandoned in favor of steel, cement, or even fiberglass tanks. These materials are also used for the watering troughs which are connected to the tanks and to the ranch houses with galvanized iron pipe or plastic pipe.

In spite of the improved access to water, drought is still a problem. Between 1900 and 1989, rainfall was well below average about thirty-six percent of the time (Norwine and Bingham 1985), forcing ranchers into critical decisions concerning future range production, cash flow, indebtedness, and herd size changes. The most common methods used by South Texas ranchers for drought management include supplemental feeding and increased culling rates, simple herd reduction, leasing more land, using more crop residue, burning prickly pear cactus to feed the cattle, and prayer (Carson, Paschal, and Hanselka 1992).

Changes in the Work and Life of the Cowboy

While cowboys on some larger ranches still spend most of their time working cattle, those on smaller ranches often spend as much or more time building fences, maintaining windmills, and other similar work. An inspection of a cowboy's pickup today will likely reveal such tools as fence stretchers, wire pliers, hammers, and even a steel post driver—tools necessary to maintaining fences. While most cowboys still ride horses and round up, rope and brand cattle, their methods differ greatly from those in the past.

The pickup truck and horse trailer make it possible for cowboys to cover far more territory than they could by horseback alone. They saddle their horses, put them in horse trailers, and drive to the area where they will work the cattle. Once the work is complete, they load

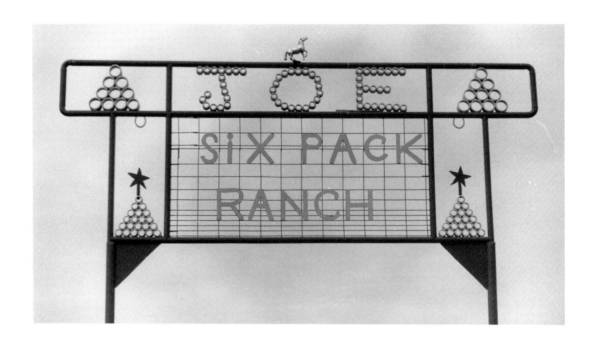

Top: Ranch entranceway made of castaway oil field pipe in Zapata County. Gateways have become a folk art in South Texas. Courtesy Joe S. Graham.

Bottom: Modern corrals on many ranches are made of used oil field pipe and drill stem, such as these on the Rancho El Niño Feliz in Zapata County. Courtesy Joe S. Graham.

Top left: In many places, the electric pump and pressure tank have replaced the windmill as a source of water for both cattle and humans. Courtesy Joe S. Graham.

Top right: Fiberglass pressure tank with pump on the Armstrong Ranch, which has replaced the windmills and hand-dug wells as a source of water for cattle. Courtesy Joe S. Graham.

Left: Modern fiberglass watering trough. Courtesy Joe S. Graham.

Top: Caterpillar completing an earthen dam, Rancho El Niño Feliz, Zapata County. When the water table is too deep to use windmills on electric pumps, ranchers dam up *arroyos*. Courtesy Joe S. Graham.

Bottom: Machine-made lake at Rancho El Niño Feliz. This fifteen-acre lake supplies water for ranch livestock and drilling companies in the region, often being piped over 20 miles. Courtesy Joe S. Graham.

Quarantine sign near the dipping vat on U.S. Highway 83 in Starr County. Courtesy Joe S. Graham.

Government dipping vat on U.S. Highway 83. Cattle must be dipped before they can legally be brought across the Rio Grande. Courtesy Joe S. Graham.

Top: A gas compressing plant in Zapata County. The gas is carried by pipeline to the nearest gas refining plant. Courtesy Joe S. Graham.

Bottom: Butane pear burners. During drouth years, cowboys burn thorns from prickly pears, transforming a nuisance into a nutritious food for hungry cattle. Courtesy King Ranch Archives.

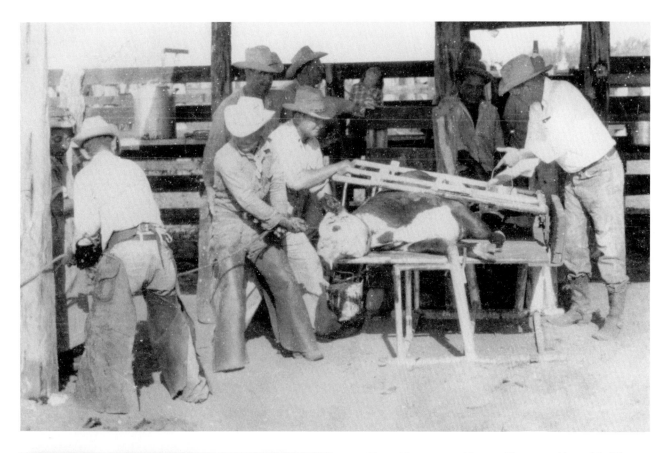

Above: Vaqueros working a calf on a marking table. The marking table reduces the effort of handling calves, replacing the processes of roping, throwing, and tying calves to be marked and branded. Courtesy King Ranch Archives.

Left: A Bob Kleberg Running W Saddle, 1989. Mexican-American saddlemakers on the King Ranch have been turning out quality saddles since 1865. Courtesy Joe S. Graham.

Right: A *vaquero* in his chaps taking a water break in the corral. Courtesy King Ranch Archives.

Facing page, top: Modern *vaqueros* with horses in a trailer attached to a pickup. This arrangement provides great mobility so the cowboy can travel many miles in a day. Courtesy Joe S. Graham.

Facing page, bottom: A roundup by helicopter on a South Texas ranch. Assisted by mounted cowboys, helicopters quickly work large pastures. Courtesy John E. Conner Museum.

Working cattle in corrals in the 1920s. Courtesy King Ranch Archives.

Men loading cattle on a train at Norias, in Kenedy County, in 1913. After the end of the open range period, cattle were driven to shipping pens along the railroads, then shipped to markets throughout the United States. Courtesy King Ranch Archives.

A dipping vat on the Norias Division of the King Ranch in the early 1900s. Courtesy King Ranch Archives.

Cattle being dipped at the Norias Division of the King Ranch in the early 1900s. Courtesy King Ranch Archives.

Top: Roping and branding livestock in an open pasture on the King Ranch. Courtesy King Ranch Archives.

Bottom: Monkey, the foundation sire of the Santa Gertrudis breed, about 1930. Courtesy King Ranch Archives.

the horses back into the trailers and drive back to ranch headquarters. Likewise, large cattle trucks have eliminated even the shorter cattle drives. Cattle to be sold are picked up directly from the ranch by these trucks and taken to distant sales barns or feed lots.

On only a few ranches, such as the Norias Division of the King Ranch, do cowboys continue to work cattle in the old way. The nature of the roundup on the majority of ranches has changed tremendously. Herded from a single pasture into modern corrals, cattle are forced into cutting chutes, loading chutes, squeeze chutes, and marking tables, making the branding, vaccinating, marking, and castrating of animals easier and requiring fewer cowboys. Over the last quarter of a century, the helicopter has had an impact on the roundups of some of the larger ranches. Assisted by mounted cowboys, the helicopter operator, in just a few hours, can complete a roundup that once would have taken days. One drawback to this system is that many cattle learn how to hide from the helicopter—in brush, ditches or tall grass—necessitating the use of *vaqueros* to find and return them to the main herd. Recently, an unbranded seven-year-old cow was discovered on the King Ranch who had escaped the helicopter roundup since birth (Cathy Henry interview).

The use of such modern devices as squeeze chutes or marking tables has greatly reduced the amount of both physical labor and dangers to which the cowboy is exposed. As herds of cattle are driven into the corrals, the calves are separated from their mothers with a cutting chute. Cowboys with *chicotes* (cattle whips) or hot shots (battery-powered devices producing an electrical shock) force the calves, one at a time, into either a squeeze chute or a chute with a marking table. This process reduces the amount of manhandling a calf must go through, as well as the number of strained muscles and/or bruises a cowboy suffers. It also means that only half the number of cowboys are needed to process the same number of calves.

Another task for the modern cowboy is to help provide food and dietary supplements for the cattle in various pastures. During drought periods and during the winter, when the grass has grown scarce, cowboys spend much of their time in pickups, carrying food to the animals, where they place it into various types of feeders. They also place salt and minerals into each pasture. On some small ranches where they cultivate prickly pear as insurance against hard times, that task also falls to the cowboys.

Modern Cowboy Accouterments

Since cowboys spend more time in pickups and afoot than they do astride horses, their boots and spurs reflect these changes. The tall riding heels on boots have begun to disappear, being replaced by the lower walking heels. Many cowboys prefer "roper" boots, with lower tops and very low heels, similar to those found on most shoes. Also, since horses are not as wild as they once were, the heavier "working" spurs are not so important. Many cowboys wear very light spurs with rowels no larger than a nickel. Younger cowboys usually prefer baseball-style caps to wide-brimmed hats. Most still wear commercial jeans and long-sleeved shirts, however, as well as bandannas to prevent sunburned necks and keep dust out. In any case, most clothing is mass-produced gear purchased in local western-wear stores, making it practically impossible to distinguish between a Mexican-American *vaquero* and an Anglo-American cowboy.

Mass-produced saddles, bridles, quirts, and chaps, costing less than their handcrafted counterparts, have mostly replaced the handmade items—although some cowboys still prefer the latter because of their link to the past. Strong, stiff nylon lariats have replaced hemp ones, which had earlier replaced the rawhide ones. *Vaqueros* in South Texas have added their own touch to this mass-produced nylon item by adding a leather or rawhide *botón,* a quick-release mechanism designed to free the lariat from the saddlehorn if the cowboy gets into trouble after roping a large animal. Other equipment that a few *vaqueros* continue to make by hand are quirts, *chicotes,* hackamores, headstalls for bridles, bridle reins, *bosales,* and *cabrestos.* Some still use rawhide, but in recent years, *vaqueros* braid many of these artifacts of slender nylon cords. *Vaqueros* on the Alta Vista Ranch also continue to make horsehair *cabrestos.*

The biggest challenge for many *vaquero* artisans, particularly those who are retired, is finding the raw materials—horsehair and rawhide—from which to make the various objects (Graham 1991b).

In years past, many South Texas communities and even some ranches had saddlemakers who developed reputations for excellence. Ready access to mass-produced saddles, which tend to be significantly cheaper than handmade ones, have led to a decline in the number of saddlemakers working in the region, although some continue their work. The King Ranch Running W Saddle Shop, producing saddles since 1865, once had as many as ten saddlemakers working fulltime; it now has only one (Graham 1991b).

Two

Modern

Ranches

El Randado: From Mexican Hacienda to Modern Ranch

Established in the 1830s by Don Hipólito and his two brothers, El Randado has undergone changes common to many ranches of Hispanic South Texas. Once a large *hacienda* of over 100,000 acres, it has been divided among family members several times and now comprises five separate ranches, the result of the division of properties among descendants. Randado, the original ranch headquarters, now consists of about 2000 acres. By the 1920s oil boom, El Randado had grown into a small, self-contained community of about 200, with a store, a post office, a school, a cotton gin, and a sugar refinery. The present owner, Don Rafael de la Garza, with the help of one *vaquero,* carries on the work of maintaining this historic ranch (Rafael de la Garza interview).

Hipólito bought a 45,000-acre Spanish land grant from Carlos Rodríguez and brought his new bride, Doña Andrea, to the new State of Tamaulipas, Mexico. As a way station in a sparsely inhabited land, El Randado entertained such visitors as General Robert E. Lee; Catarino Garza, a Governor of Tamaulipas once branded an outlaw by the State of Texas; and members of the 8th U.S. Calvary and the Texas Rangers. In the 1850s, the ranch headquarters was a self-contained community. It produced almost everything needed for the ranch and its people (Casstevens 1991).

Two Social Classes

House architecture at Randado reflected the social structure on the ranch. The *casas mayores* were built of *sillares,* with floors and flat roofs of *chipichil.* Doors and shuttered windows, placed to insure a good cross breeze in each room, were made of handcarved mesquite. Door hinges, latches, and keys were made by the ranch blacksmiths. Don Hipólito and Doña Andrea raised their family in a large two-story house. It was used as a dwelling until the 1930s, when it was converted to a cotton gin, a purpose it served until 1947. In 1967, it was torn down and the blocks used to build a fence around the home of Sarita Kenedy East (Casstevens 1991). The house built for Doña Margarita de la Garza, the García's only child (an adopted daughter), was greatly modified in the 1950s. Modern glass windows replaced the originally shuttered, glass-less openings, a front porch with a clay tile roof was added, and plumbing and electricity were put in. Although it is still standing today, this house has been vacant for many years (Casstevens 1991).

The working-class folk at Randado lived in *jacales de leña,* whose steeply pitched thatched roofs made it possible to add rooms to the gabled ends of the *jacales,* but not on the sides. Because the walls were eight to ten inches thick and plastered with mud or lime mortar, the houses were very comfortable. As on other ranches, this type of architecture disappeared from Randado by the 1950s and the buildings were not

Top: Dueña's Palace at El Randado headquarters, about 1930. The Garcías raised their family in this large two-story house. From 1930–1947 it housed a cotton gin. In 1967 it was torn down and the blocks used to build a fence around the home of Sarita Kenedy East. Photo was taken in the 1930s. Courtesy de la Garza Family Archives.

Bottom: A *jacal de leña* (*jacal* of cut mesquite) at the ranch headquarters at El Randado, about 1930. *Vaqueros* and their families lived in these houses until the 1950s. Photo was taken in the 1930s. Courtesy de la Garza Family Archives.

The interior of the San Rafael Chapel at the headquarters of El Randado, completed in 1836. Benches and confessional are handcarved wood. The fourteen stations of the cross, frosted chromolithographs, and other religious images were provided by the *dueña* and subsequent families. Photo taken 1991. Courtesy Joe S. Graham.

Doña Andrea García sent to Paris, France, for this statue of her favorite saint, the archangel San Rafael (St. Raphael), about 1850. Courtesy Joe S. Graham.

The family cemetery of the descendants of the owners of the Randado Ranch in Jim Hogg County, enclosed in a wrought iron fence. García Family members are buried in the cemetery to this day. Courtesy Joe S. Graham.

The cemetery of the *vaqueros* and laborers and their families on El Randado, separate from the cemetery of the landowning family. Their simple grave markers reflect their lower social status. Courtesy Joe S. Graham.

Top: Storehouse at Randado, built in the 1840s. This structure first served as a general store, then a U.S. Post Office from 1882 until 1959, and it is now a storage room for saddles, tack, and other ranch equipment. Courtesy Joe S. Graham.

Bottom: This earthen *presa* (dam) at Randado Ranch in Jim Hogg County was built in the 1830s, creating a reservoir of about five acres to water the large herds of cattle on the ranch. The dam was made by hand, using rawhide *mecapales* and *guaripas* to haul earth from in front of the dam to scatter it along the top. Courtesy Joe S. Graham.

Top: Water tank of *sillares* at Randado, built in the late 1800s. Storage tanks such as this one were found on many early ranches throughout south Texas. Courtesy Joe S. Graham.

Left: Electric pump and pressure tank at Randado. This modern unit replaced the windmill on many cattle ranches. Courtesy Joe S. Graham.

Right: Cypress tank at Randado, built in the 1940s to supply households with water. Courtesy Joe S. Graham.

Below: Modern windmill at Randado. The first windmill at the ranch headquarters was erected in 1932, set over a hand-dug well. Courtesy Joe S. Graham.

Earthen dam at Rancho La Union near San Ygnacio in
Zapata County, built in the 1850s and 1860s by laborers under
the supervision of José María and Manuel María Uribe.
Thirty feet high and about 300 feet long, it provided water
for livestock on the Martínez Ranch, where even the oldest
people do not recall it ever drying up. Courtesy Joe S.
Graham.

replaced with modern structures because of the great reduction in the population of the ranch headquarters (Casstevens 1991).

As *dueña* of the ranch, Doña Andrea saw to the building of Randado's chapel and dedicated it to the archangel St. Rafael. Benches and a confessional were handmade of wood. The fourteen stations of the cross, frosted chromolithographs, and other religious images were provided by the *dueña* and subsequent families. Doña Andrea sent to Paris, France, for a statue of San Rafael. Oral history claims that the bell in the chapel tower was cast in Corpus Christi with various precious metals from jewelry belonging to the ranch residents. The chapel was used by the priest of the region, who visited once or twice a year to conduct masses and perform weddings, baptisms, and *quinceañeras*. It was also used for prayers and other devotions of the *patrón*'s family. Over the years, structural changes have been made: a small wooden room was added to the side for the visiting priest to stay in, and the bell tower was lowered in 1929. The original thatch roof of native grasses was replaced with wooden shingles and then a metal roof. The chapel has continued to be used, and in 1988, funeral services were held there for Doña Berta, wife of the present owner of Randado (Casstevens 1991).

Another structure still in use on the ranch first served as a general store, then as a U.S. Post Office from 1882 until 1959. It is now a storage room for saddles, tack, and other ranch equipment, as well as feed, salt and minerals for the 100 or so head of cattle presently on the ranch. There are also two cemeteries on the ranch which continue to be used, both reflecting the ranch's social structure. To this day, descendants of the original García family are buried in the family cemetery, enclosed in a wrought-iron fence. *Vaqueros* and other laborers and their families were buried nearby in the workers' cemetery, where their simple grave markers reflect their lower social status (Casstevens 1991 and Rafael de la Garza interview).

The Search for Water at Randado

Randado's ranch headquarters was established alongside a dry arroyo, which would be dammed in the 1830s to create one of the first artificial lakes in South Texas. The dam, which created a five-acre lake, was constructed by ranch laborers working under the owner's direction. Using methods common in Mexico, they carried loads of dirt in *guaripas*. The earth was dumped along the dam site and packed down with herds of sheep and goats. The front of the dam and spillway were lined with *sillares*. After 150 years, the dam is still used to water cattle (Graham 1992).

Hand-dug wells, some as deep as ninety feet and lined with caliche blocks, furnished water for the many households on the ranch, although the "big houses" were designed to catch and store rainwater. The first windmill at the ranch headquarters was erected in 1932, set over a hand-dug well, and from then on windmills gradually replaced all the buckets and pulleys. The first storage tanks on Randado were made of caliche blocks, a type found on many early ranches throughout South Texas. In the 1940s, a cypress storage tank was built, and more recently, an electric pump with a pressure tank has become an important source of water for the ranch (Rafael de la Garza interview).

Alta Vista: A Modern Cattle Ranch

Unlike the Texas-Mexican *haciendas* and older ranches, which were self-sufficient, independent communities, the modern South Texas ranch is marked by close links to local communities and the outside world via telephone and automobile, as well as a cluster of other modern technologies. One of three ranches belonging to the Jones family in Jim Hogg County, the Alta Vista Ranch (acquired by A. C. Jones in 1882) continues to rely principally on cattle for its income, although the numbers of cattle and horses depends on the moisture conditions. The ranch's goal is to raise one cow per twenty acres and to produce an eighty percent calf crop (i.e., eighty percent of the cows would give birth to and raise calves). Since the same *vaqueros* work together on all three Jones ranches during round-ups and shipping, the same horses are used for all three also. With the introduction of new technologies, including pickups and horse trailers, the number of horses used has decreased from about 125 in the 1960s to 48 in 1992 (Frank Graham interview).

The sources of ranch income vary also: during drought periods, about sixty percent of the ranch income comes from the sale of livestock and forty percent comes from hunting; during years of much rain and good grass, seventy-five percent of the ranch income will be from sales of livestock and twenty-five percent from hunting.

The Alta Vista Ranch consists of about 38,000 acres divided into ten large and mid-sized pastures and ten smaller "traps," small pastures used to keep animals while they are being worked. These pastures and traps are watered by twenty-three windmills. Each windmill has a tank reservoir which feeds one or more watering troughs. Dirt roads lead to each windmill and make each pasture readily available to someone in a pickup truck. Three sets of corrals serve the whole ranch. The oldest ones, made of wire and cut lumber, are used only occasionally. The older parts of the main corrals, which have recently been remodeled, are made of heavy posts of railroad ties with horizontal planks of heavy lumber. During 1991–92, the foremen and *vaqueros* on all three of the Jones ranches, aided by a professional welder from a nearby community, gathered to build a very modern set of corrals, made of the same materials used as guardrails across creeks along Texas highways.

The most important part of these new corrals is the hydraulic squeeze chute at its center, designed and built in Weatherford, Oklahoma, by the W. C. Pigg Company, which has significantly changed the way the cattle are handled. It has also changed the number of *vaqueros* required to handle the cattle on the ranch. Twenty-five years ago, twenty cowboys worked on the ranch during roundups. In 1992, there were only twelve doing the same work (Frank Graham interview).

The ranch holds two roundups each year, one in the spring and one in the fall. The spring roundup (which begins in late April or early May and lasts until early July) is done to mark, brand, castrate, and vaccinate the calves on the ranch. The fall roundup (which begins in October and lasts through December) is done to work those calves missed in the spring roundup and to separate and ship selected animals to market. Every year or two, the bulls are rounded up and tested for fertility, a task which would have been impossible before the advent of the squeeze chutes. The ranch foreman, Frank Graham, owns over a hundred Longhorn cattle, and these animals are worked during the fall roundup to choose those ready for market.

Cowboys on the Alta Vista no longer rope and brand cattle in the open pastures; they drive them by horseback to the main corrals at the ranch headquarters. The activity in the corrals depends on what needs to be done to the animals being worked. In one roundup which took place in November, 1992, thirteen men ran 463 heifer calves through a cutting chute to separate those which would be shipped to a feedlot from those which would be kept on the ranch. Once the calves were separated into different pens, they were run through the squeeze chute one at a time, branded, given a single vaccination to protect them from eight different diseases (including blackleg, malignant edema, shipping fever, sordeli and other bovine diseases), earmarked and/or tagged, had their horns cut (in some instances), and were injected in the stomach to eliminate parasites. It took just under eight hours to process the 463 animals. Each man knows his task and does it efficiently. Fifty years ago, it would have taken the same number of cowboys a long day to do the same work on a third of these animals. Once all of the animals are processed, some are loaded onto the large trucks waiting to carry the animals to the feed pens or to another Jones ranch. Those to stay on the ranch will be driven back to the pasture they came from.

During the time *vaqueros* are not working cattle, they are helping maintain the ranch, including the twenty-three windmills and miles of barbed-wire fences. They also help maintain the equipment used on the ranch, including their own saddles and other equipment, as well as such items as the horse trailers (Frank Graham interview). Some of the *vaqueros,* led by Mariano Martínez and two of his sons, still make horsehair ropes. When they have enough horsehair, they take the handmade equipment, including a *hiladera* to twist the horsehair into long strands, the *tarango* to hold four of strands of horsehair so they can be twisted into a rope, and the *tarabilla* to do the actual twisting. The four strands are controlled and guided into a smooth twist with a handcarved *piloncillo* or *dulce* (Graham 1991b).

The *vaqueros* live on the ranch five or six days a week, depending on the work going on at the time, and on weekends drive to town to be with their families. While the families of most live in nearby Hebbronville, which is just twenty-five miles away, Mariano's family lives in Rio Grande City, a distance of over forty miles. While on the ranch, the *vaqueros* live in a fairly spacious bunkhouse, which they are responsible for keeping clean. It is equipped with numerous beds and a restroom with showers. They eat together in the screened-in kitchen/dining room nearby. The food is prepared by the ranch cook, who prepares mostly traditional Mexican-American dishes common on ranches in the area—flour tortillas, *carne guisada, taquitos* of various types, hot coffee, etc. The cook rises very early to prepare the *vaqueros'* breakfast, particularly when they

are working cattle. Once breakfast is completed, he cleans up and begins work on the noon meal.

While the bunkhouse and the kitchen/dining room are located near the main working corrals and the large barns and storage sheds, the other houses at the ranch headquarters are about a half-mile away. The oldest of these houses at the headquarters, built in 1904, is the home of the ranch foreman, Frank Graham (W. W. Jones interview). Other houses provide shelter for the families of the men who do the maintenance on the ranch headquarters. Two homes are used by members of the ranch owners who come to the ranch from time to time.

In essence, these cowboys and others like them on modern ranches in South Texas are cultural descendants of the earliest *vaqueros* who came to Texas with the first herds of Spanish cattle. Although their methods of work have changed significantly and they have adapted their costume, equipment and work methods to the demands of new technologies, the men on horseback are still essential to ranch work. Without them, modern ranches like the Alta Vista would not exist. Together, the ranch and the cowboy represent a major Spanish/Mexican contribution to the culture and economy not only of South Texas but of American culture in general, particularly that of the West and Southwest.

Right: Frank Graham, foreman on the Alta Vista Ranch. Courtesy Joe S. Graham.

Below: The Alta Vista *vaqueros* from left to right: Gonzalo Santos, Acario Castillo, José Domínguez, Giliberto Domínguez, Martín De Anda, Frank Graham (ranch foreman), Rito Martínez, David Lee Henry (foreman on the Alto Colorado Ranch), Mariano Martínez, and Rolando Silguero. Courtesy Joe S. Graham.

Top: Modern cowboy working cattle on the Alta Vista Ranch. Courtesy W. W. Jones Family Archives.

Bottom: Vaqueros driving a herd of cattle to the corrals on the Alta Vista Ranch. Courtesy W. W. Jones Family Archives.

Top: Cowboys loading cattle onto one of the first pickups with a stock trailer on the Alta Vista Ranch in the 1950s. Courtesy W. W. Jones Family Archives.

Bottom: One of the first four-wheel-drive pickups and stock trailers on the Alta Vista Ranch. Photo taken in the early 1950s. Courtesy W. W. Jones Family Archives.

Top: Saddle horses loaded on a modern goose-neck trailer on the Alta Vista Ranch. Courtesy Joe S. Graham.

Bottom: Alta Vista cowboys' pickups and autos. Courtesy Joe S. Graham.

Hunters on the Alta Vista ranch have been successful.

Hunting is an important source of income on most ranches

in the region. Courtesy W. W. Jones Family Archives.

Left: The windmill, part of 1980s watering system on Alta Vista Ranch. Courtesy Joe S. Graham.

Below: The dirt tank, part of 1980s watering system on Alta Vista Ranch. Courtesy Joe S. Graham.

Top: Alta Vista *vaqueros* branding calves in the corrals in the 1950s. Courtesy W. W. Jones Family Archives.

Bottom: Alta Vista *vaqueros* rounding up cattle in the 1950s. Courtesy W. W. Jones Family Archives.

Cowboys on the Alta Vista Ranch making horsehair rope. Courtesy Joe S. Graham.

Above and on facing page: Closeups of cowboys making horsehair rope. Courtesy Joe S. Graham.

Closeups of cowboys making horsehair rope. Courtesy Joe S. Graham.

Closeups of cowboys making horsehair rope.Courtesy Joe S. Graham.

Bibliography

Books and Articles

Adams, Andy. 1903. *Log of a Cowboy.* Lincoln: University of Nebraska Press.

Adams, Ramon. 1944. *Western Words.* Norman: University of Oklahoma Press.

———. 1950. *The Cowman & His Code of Ethics.* Austin: Encino Press.

———. 1964. *The Rampaging Herd.* Norman: University of Oklahoma Press.

Ahlborn, Richard E., ed. 1980. *Man Made Mobile: Early Saddles of Western North America.* Washington, D.C.: Smithsonian Institution Press.

Akerman, Joe A., Jr. 1976. *Florida Cowman: A History of Florida Cattle Raising.* Kissimmee: Florida Cattlemen's Association.

Alonzo, Armando C. 1991. "Tejano Rancheros: Changes in Land Tenure, Hidalgo County, 1850–1900." Unpublished Ph.D. Dissertation, Indiana University, Bloomington.

Atherton, Lewis E. 1961. *The Cattle Kings.* Bloomington: Indiana University Press.

Axelrod, Alan, ed. 1989. *Ranching Traditions: Legacy of the American West.* New York: Abbeville Press.

Baker, T. Lindsay. 1992. *Blades in the Sky.* Lubbock: Texas Tech University Press.

Beatie, Russell H. 1981. *Saddles.* Norman: University of Oklahoma Press.

Beckstead, James H. 1991. *Cowboying: A Tough Job in a Hard Land.* Salt Lake City: University of Utah Press.

Berlandier, Jean L. 1980. *Journey to Mexico during the Years 1826 to 1834.* Translated by Sheila M. Ohlendorf et al.; edited by C. H. Muller et al. 2 vols. Austin: Texas State Historical Association.

Bishko, Charles J. 1952. "The Peninsular Background of Latin American Cattle Ranching." *The Hispanic American Historical Review* XXXII (4): 491–515.

Brand, Donald D. 1961. "The Early History of the Range Cattle Industry in Northern Mexico." *Agricultural History* XXXV: 132–139.

Carson, William, Joe C. Paschal and Wayne Hanselka. 1992. "Successful Ranches in South Texas, A Profile of Integrated Resource Management in the Rio Grande Plains." Corpus Christi: Texas Agriculture Extension Service.

Casstevens, Mary A. 1991. "Randado: The Built Environment of a Texas-Mexican Ranch." In Joe S. Graham, ed., *Hecho en Tejas: Texas-Mexican Folk Arts and Crafts.* Denton: University of North Texas Press. Publications of the Texas Folklore Society 50, pp. 309–334.

Castañeda, Carlos E. 1936–58. *Our Catholic Heritage in Texas.* 7 vols. Austin: Von Boeckmann-Jones Co.

Chevalier, François. 1963. *Land and Society in Colonial Mexico-The Great Hacienda.* Berkeley: University of California Press.

Choate, Julian E., Jr., and Joe B. Frantz. 1955. *The American Cowboy.* Norman: University of Oklahoma Press.

Coolidge, Dana. 1937. *Texas Cowboys.* New York: E.P. Dutton and Co.

Cox, James 1895. *Historical and Biographical Record of the Cattle Industry and the Cattlemen of Texas and Adjacent Territory.* Saint Louis: Woodward and Tiernan Printing Co.

Dale, Edward E. 1930. *The Range Cattle Industry.* Norman: University of Oklahoma Press.

Dary, David. 1981. *Cowboy Culture: A Saga of Five Centuries.* Lawrence: University Press of Kansas.

De León, Arnoldo. 1979. "Rancheros, Comerciantes, and Trabajadores in South Texas, 1848–1900." In Margarita B. Melville, ed., *Reflections of the Mexican Experience in Texas.* Houston: Mexican American Studies Center, University of Houston.

———. 1982. *The Tejano Community, 1836–1900*. Albuquerque: University of New Mexico Press.

———. 1983. *They Called Them Greasers: Anglo Attitudes Toward Mexicans in Texas, 1921–1900*. Austin: University of Texas Press.

——— and K. L. Stewart. 1983. "Lost Dreams and Found Fortunes: Mexican and Anglo Immigrants to South Texas, 1850–1900." *Western Historical Quarterly* 14(3): 291–310.

De Solís, Gaspar José. 1931. "Diary of Fray Gaspar José de Solís, in the Year 1767–68." *Southwestern Historical Quarterly* XXXV: 28–76. (Tr. by Margaret Kenney Kress).

Denhardt, Robert M. 1975. *The Horse of the Americas*. Norman: University of Oklahoma Press.

Dobie, J. Frank. 1929. A *Vaquero of the Brush Country*. Dallas: The Southwest Press.

———. 1939. "The First Cattle in Texas and the Southwest Progenitors of the Longhorns." *Southwestern Historical Quarterly* XLII (3): 171–197.

———. 1941. *The Longhorns*. Boston: Little, Brown and Co.

———. 1952. *The Mustangs*. Boston: Little, Brown and Co.

———. 1964. *Cow People*. Boston: Little Brown and Co.

Dusenberry, William. H. 1963. *The Mexican Mesta, The Administration of Ranching in Colonial Mexico*. Urbana: University of Illinois Press.

Fish, Jean Y. 1991. *José Vásquez Borrego and La Hacienda de Nuestra Señora de Dolores*. Zapata: Zapata County Historical Society.

Ford, Gus L., ed. 1936. *Texas Cattle Brands*. Dallas: Clyde C. Cockrell Co.

Fugate, Francis L. 1961. "Origins of the Range Cattle Era in South Texas." *Agricultural History* XXXV: 155–158.

García, Clotilde P. 1984. *Captain Blás Mariá de la Garza Falcón: Colonizer of South Texas*. Corpus Christi: Grunvald Printing Co.

———. 1986. *Captain Enrique Villarreal and the Rincon del Oso Land Grant*. Corpus Christi: Grunvald Printing Co.

García, Rogelia E. 1970. *Dolores, Revilla, and Laredo: Three Sister Settlements*. Waco: Texian Press.

George, Eugene. 1975. *Historic Architecture of Texas: The Falcon Reservoir*. Austin: Texas Historical Commission.

Gilliland, Maude. 1964. *Rincon (Remote Dwelling Place): A Story of Life on a South Texas Ranch at the Turn of the Century*. Brownsville: Springman-King Lithograph Co.

González, Jovita. 1927. "Folk-lore of the Texas-Mexican Vaquero." In J. Frank Dobie, ed. *Texas and Southwestern Lore*. Publications of the Texas Folklore Society VI. Austin: Texas Folklore Society, pp. 7–22.

———. 1930. "Social Life in Cameron, Starr, and Zapata Counties." Master's Thesis, University of Texas, Austin.

———. 1932. "Among My People." In J. Frank Dobie, ed., *Tone the Bell Easy*. Publications of the Texas Folklore Society X. Austin: Texas Folklore Society, pp. 99–108.

Goodwyn, Frank. 1951. *Life on the King Ranch*. New York: Thomas Y. Crowell Co.

Graf, LeRoy P. 1942. "The Economic History of the Lower Rio Grande Valley 1820–1875." Unpublished Ph.D. Dissertation, Harvard University.

Graham, Joe. S. 1978. "Folk Housing in South and West Texas: Some Comparisons." In Marlene Heck, ed., *An Exploration of a Common Legacy*. Austin: Texas Historical Commission, pp. 36–53.

———. 1985. "Folk Medicine and Intracultural Diversity Among West Texas Mexican Americans." *Western Folklore* XLIV (3): 168–193.

———. 1988. "The Jacal in the Big Bend: Its Origin and Evolution." In Robert J. Mallouf, ed., *Contributed Papers of the Second Symposium on Resources of the Chihuahuan Desert Region*, Chihuahuan Desert Research Institute Publication #20, Alpine, Tex.

———. 1991a. "Hecho a mano en Tejas." In Joe S. Graham, ed., *Hecho en Tejas: Texas-Mexican Folk Arts and Crafts*. Denton: University of North Texas Press. Publications of the Texas Folklore Society 50, pp. 1–47.

———. 1991b. "Vaquero Folk Arts and Crafts Traditions in South Texas." In Joe S. Graham, ed., *Hecho en Tejas: Texas-Mexican Folk Arts and Crafts*. Denton: University of North Texas Press. Publications of the Texas Folklore Society 50, pp. 93–116.

———. 1991c. "The *Jacal* in South Texas: The Origins and Form of a Folk House." In Joe S. Graham, ed., *Hecho en Tejas: Texas-Mexican Folk Arts and Crafts*. Denton: University of North Texas Press. Publications of the Texas Folklore Society 50, pp. 293–308.

———. 1992. "The Built Environment in South Texas: The Hispanic Legacy." In Helen Simmons and Cathryn A. Hoyt, eds., *Hispanic Texas: A Historical Guide*. Austin: University of Texas Press, pp. 58–75.

———. 1993 "The History of Cattle Ranching in South Texas." In H. Russell Cross, ed., *Partners in Progress Since 1891*. College Station: Texas A&M University Dept. of Animal Science, pp. B1-B22.

———. In press. "The Hispanic Heritage of Ranching in South Texas." In Kenneth Davis, ed., *International Cowboy Symposium*. Lubbock: Texas Tech University Press.

Grimm, Agnes. 1968. *Llanos Mesteños: Mustang Plains*. Waco: Texian Press.

Guide to Spanish and Mexican Land Grants in South Texas.

1988. Austin: General Land Office, Garry Mauro, Land Commissioner.

Haley, J. Evetts, ed. 1932. "A Log of the Texas-California Cattle Trail, 1854, James G. Bell." *Southwestern Historical Quarterly* XXXV (3): 208–211.

———. 1936. *Charles Goodnight, Cowman and Plainsman.* Boston: Houghton Mifflin Co.

———. 1952. *Life on the Texas Range.* Austin: University of Texas Press.

Herrington, George S. 1951. "An Early Cattle Drive from Texas to Illinois." *Southwestern Historical Quarterly* LV(2): 267–269.

Hinojosa, Gilberto N. 1983. *A Borderlands Town in Transition: Laredo, Texas, 1775–1870.* College Station: Texas A&M University Press.

Holden, William C. 1934. *The Spur Ranch.* Boston: Christopher Publishing House.

Hoyt, Cathryn A. 1992. "Riches, Religion, and Politics: Early Exploration in Texas." In Helen Simmons and Cathryn A. Hoyt, eds., *Hispanic Texas: A Historical Guide.* Austin: University of Texas Press, pp. 13–24.

Hughes, George W. 1849–50. *Memoir Descriptive of a Division of the United States Army,* under the command of Brigadier General John G. Wool, from San Antonio de Bexar, in Texas, to Saltillo, in Mexico, Sen. Ex. Doc. No. 32, 31st Cong., 1st Session.

Jackson, Jack. 1986. *Los Mesteños: Spanish Ranching in Texas 1721–1821.* College Station: Texas A&M University Press.

Jacobs, Ian. 1982. *Ranchero Revolt.* Austin: University of Texas Press.

Jordan, Teresa. 1982. *Cowgirls: Women of the American West.* Garden City, NY: Anchor Press.

Jordan, Terry C. 1981. *Trails to Texas: Southern Roots of Western Cattle Ranching.* Lincoln: University of Nebraska Press.

Ladewig, H., D. G. Warren, R. A. Rupp, and J. R. Beverly. 1984. *South Texas Integrated Beef Herd Improvement Program.* College Station: Texas Agricultural Extension Service, Texas Agricultural Experiment Station.

Lea, Tom. 1957. *The King Ranch.* 2 vols. Boston: Little, Brown and Co.

Lehmann, Valgene W. 1969. *Forgotten Legions: Sheep in the Rio Grande Plain of Texas.* El Paso: Texas Western Press.

Lott, Virgil N. and Mercurio Martínez. 1953. *Kingdom of Zapata.* San Antonio: Naylor Co.

Lomax, John A. 1967. *Cow Camps & Cattle Herds.* Austin: Encino Press.

Love, Clara M. 1916. "History of the Cattle Industry in the Southwest." *Southwestern Historical Quarterly,* XIX: 370–399.

Machado, Manuel A., Jr. 1981. *The North Mexican Cattle Industry, 1910–1975.* College Station: Texas A&M University Press.

McCoy, Joseph G. 1874. *Historic Sketches of the Cattle Trade of the West and Southwest.* Kansas City: Ramsey, Millett and Hudson.

McMurtry, Larry. 1985. *Lonesome Dove.* New York: Simon and Schuster.

Meinig, D.W. 1969. *Imperial Texas: An Interpretation Essay in Cultural Geography.* Austin: University of Texas Press.

Miller, Hubert F. 1980. *José de Escandón: Colonizer of Nuevo Santander.* Edinburg: The New Santander Press.

Montejano, David. 1987. *Anglos and Mexicans in the Making of Texas, 1836–1986.* Austin: University of Texas Press.

Mora, Jo. 1946. *Trail Dust and Saddle Leather.* New York: Charles Scribner's Sons.

———. 1949. *Californios.* Garden City: Doubleday and Co.

Morrisey, Richard J. 1949. "The Establishment and Northward Expansion of Cattle Ranching in New Spain." Unpublished Ph.D. Dissertation, University of California, Berkeley.

———. 1950. "The Early Range Cattle Industry in Arizona." *Agricultural History* XXIV: 151–156.

———. 1951. "The Northward Expansion of Cattle Ranching in New Spain, 1550–1600." *Agricultural History* XXV: 115–121.

———. 1957. "Colonial Agriculture in New Spain." *Agricultural History* XXXI: 24–29.

Myres, Sandra L. 1966. "The Spanish Cattle Kingdom in the Province of Texas." *Texana* IV: 233–246.

———. 1969. *The Ranch in Spanish Texas, 1691–1800.* El Paso: Texas Western Press.

Nordyke, Lewis. 1955. *Great Roundup: The Story of Texas and Southwestern Cowmen.* New York: Morrow and Co.

Norwine, James and R. Bingham. 1985. "Frequency and Severity of Droughts in South Texas: 1900–1983." In *Proceedings of Symposium, Livestock and Wildlife Management During Drought,* Kingsville, Texas. College Station: Texas Agricultural Extension Service, pp. 1–117.

Nueces County Historical Society, Comp. 1972. *The History of Nueces County.* Austin: Jenkins Publishing Co.

Olmsted, Frederick L. 1857. *A Journey through Texas; Or, a Saddle-Trip on the Southwestern Border.* New York: Dix, Edwards & Co. Reprint, Austin: University of Texas Press, 1978.

Paredes, Américo. 1958. *"With His Pistol in His Hand": A Border Ballad and Its Hero.* Austin: University of Texas Press.

Ramírez, Emilia S. 1971. *Ranch Life in Hidalgo County after 1850.* Edinburg: New Santander Press.

Ramírez, Norma E. 1979. "The Vaquero and Ranching in the Southwestern United States, 1600 to 1970." Unpublished Ph.D. Dissertation, Indiana University, Bloomington.

Ramón, Ildefonso. 1835. Letter to Governor of Tamaulipas, Laredo Archives.

Rice, Lee M. and Glenn R. Vernam. 1975. *They Saddled the West*. Cambridge: Cornell Maritime Press.

Richardson, R. H. 1978. *The Screwworm Problem*. Austin: University of Texas Press.

Robertson, Brian. 1985. *Wild Horse Desert*. Edinburg: New Santander Press.

Rocha, Rodolfo. 1974. "Background to Banditry in the Lower Rio Grande Valley of Texas, 1900–1912." Unpublished M.A. Thesis, Pan American University, Edinburg, Texas.

Rojas, Arnold R. 1964. *The Vaquero*. Charlotte and Santa Barbara: McNally and Loftin.

Rouse, John E. 1977. *The Criollo: Spanish Cattle in the Americas*. Norman: University of Oklahoma Press.

Rubio, Abel G. 1986. *Stolen Heritage: A Mexican American's Rediscovery of His Family's Lost Land*. Edited with a foreword by Thomas H. Kreneck. Austin: University of Texas Press.

Rubio, Victor J. M. 1982. *La vivienda indígena de México y del mundo*. Mexico City: Universidad Nacional Autonoma de Mexico.

Salinas, Martín. 1990. *Indians of the Rio Grande Delta*. Austin: University of Texas Press.

Sánchez, Mario L., ed. 1991. *A Shared Experience*. Austin: Texas: Historical Commission.

Sandoz, Mari. 1958. *The Cattlemen: From the Rio Grande Across the Far Marias*. New York: Hastings House.

Schell, William Jr. 1988. *Medieval Iberian Tradition and the Development of the Mexican Hacienda*. Syracuse: Foreign and Comparative Studies/Latin American Series, No. 8. Maxwell School of Citizenship and Public Affairs, Syracuse University.

Scott, Florence. J. 1937. *Historical Heritage of the Lower Rio Grande Valley. 1747–1848*. San Antonio: Naylor Co. Revised edition, 1966, Waco: Texian Press.

———. 1969. *Royal Land Grants North of the Rio Grande, 1777–1821*. Rio Grande City: La Retama Press.

Shelton, Emily J. 1947. "Lizzie E. Johnson: A Cattle Queen of Texas." *Southwestern Historical Quarterly* L: 349–366.

Simmons, Helen and Cathryn A. Hoyt, eds., 1992. *Hispanic Texas: A Historical Guide*. Austin: University of Texas Press.

Simmons, Ozzie G. 1974. *Anglo-Americans and Mexican-Americans in South Texas*. New York: Arno Press.

Siringo, Charles A. 1885. *A Texas Cowboy*. Chicago: Umbdenstock and Co.

Smith, Diane S. 1986. *The Armstrong Chronicle: A Ranching History*. San Antonio: Corona Publishing Co.

Sonnichsen, C.L. 1950. *Cowboys and Cattle Kings: Life on the Range Today*. Norman: University of Oklahoma Press.

Sweet, Alexander E. and John A. Knox. 1883. *On a Mexican Mustang through Texas: From the Gulf to the Rio Grande*. Hartford: S.S. Scranton & Co.

Taylor, Lonn and Ingrid Marr. 1983. *The American Cowboy*. Washington, D.C.: American Folklife Center, Library of Congress.

Taylor, Virginia H., comp. 1974. *Index to Spanish and Mexican Land Grants in Texas*. Austin: Lone Star Press.

Thompson, Jerry D. 1974. *Sabers on the Rio Grande*. Austin: Presidial Press.

———. 1976. *Vaqueros in Blue and Gray*. Austin: Presidial Press.

Thonhoff, Robert H. 1964. "The First Ranch in Texas." *West Texas Historical Association Yearbook* XXXX: 90–97.

Tijerina, Andrew A. 1977. "Tejanos and Texas: The Native Mexicans of Texas, 1820–1850." Unpublished Ph.D. dissertation, University of Texas, Austin.

Vernam, Glenn R. 1964. *Man on Horseback*. New York: Harper and Row.

Villarreal, Roberto M. 1970. "The Mexican-American Vaqueros of the Kenedy Ranch: A Social History." Unpublished M.A. thesis, Texas A&I University.

Wagoner, Junior J. 1952. *History of the Cattle Industry in Southern Arizona, 1540–1940*. Tucson: University of Arizona Press.

Ward, Fay E. 1958. *The Cowboy at Work*. New York: Hastings House.

Webb, Walter P. 1931. *The Great Plains*. Boston: Ginn and Company.

Weddle, Robert S. 1992. "Cross and Crown: The Spanish Missions in Texas." In Helen Simmons and Cathryn A. Hoyt, eds., *Hispanic Texas: A Historical Guide*. Austin: University of Texas Press, pp. 25–36.

Wilcox, Seb S. 1938. "Laredo During the Texas Republic." *Southwestern Historical Quarterly* XLII(2): 83–107.

Wilkinson, J.B. 1975. *Laredo and the Rio Grande Frontier*. Austin: Jenkins Co.

Wolf, Eric and Sidney W. Mintz. 1957. "Haciendas and Plantations in Middle America and the Antilles." *Social & Economic Studies* 6: 380–412.

Worcester, Don. 1987. *The Texas Longhorn: Relic of the Past, Asset for the Future*. College Station: Texas A&M University Press.

Interviewees

Joaquín Arredondo
Alberto Barrera
Bruce Cheeseman
Rafael de la Garza
Martín Dimas
Rubén Éscobar
Adalberto Garza
Shirley Gonzáles
Frank Graham
Enrique Guerra
Diego Gutiérrez
Doniciano "Chanate" Gutiérrez
"Mundi" Gutiérrez
Cathy Henry
W. W. Jones
José Roberto Juárez
Robert King
Acela Martínez
Adrian Martínez
Guadalupe Martínez
Mariano Martínez
Jim McAllen
Tommy Molina
Miguel Muñiz
R. G. Sánchez
Alberto "Lolo" Treviño
Rosa Nelia Treviño

Index

Abilene, Kansas, 40, 41
agriculture, 7, 9, 15–16, 29, 56–57, 60, 66–67, 70, 86
Alamo River, 19
Alfonso VI of León-Castile, 9
Alfonso VII of León-Castile, 9
Allen, John, 37
Alta Vista Ranch, 52, 56, 58, 69, 70, 83, 95–109
altars, 25, 28
Alto Colorado Ranch, 98
Anda, Martín de, 98
architecture, 19, 49, 52–53, 85, 95, 97; *bancas*, 31; board-and-batten, 54; bunkhouses, 49, 97; *casas mayores*, 24, 26, 31, 32, 33, 39, 85, 86; *chimeneas*, 26; *hacienda*, 16–17; headquarters, 39, 85; *horcones*, 31; *jacales*, 14, 21, 25, 31, 39, 54, 85, 86; *ramadas*, 25; storehouses, 91; *troneras* (gunports), 26, 31, 32, 42
Armstrong, John, 52
Armstrong Ranch, 38, 39, 41, 44, 50, 51, 62, 73
arts and crafts, 26, 28, 42, 84

Ballí, José María de, 23
Ballí, Juan José, 23
Ballí, Rosa María Hinojosa de, 23
Ballí family, 39
"band of brothers," 37
bandidos, 15
Bazán family, 39, 49
Benavida, Juan Alfonso de, 9
Benavides, Luciano, 37
Béxar, 37
Bishko, Charles J., 9
Bishop, Texas, 66
bison, 13, 15
Black Friday, 40
blacksmiths, 42, 49

Borrego, Bartholome, 20
Borrego, José Vásquez de, 20, 21, 25
Borrego, Juan José, 21
Borrego, Macario, 21
Borrego, Manuela, 21–22
Borrego, Miguel, 21
Borrego heirs, 20, 21
Borrego land grant, 20–22
Bourland Commission, 20
branding. *See* livestock
brands, 12; registration, 12; trail, 29
Brazos River, 8
Brooks County, 38
Browne, Lieutenant, 37
Brownsville, Texas, 26, 38, 39, 51, 52, 66
Bruni, Anthony Mateo, 22
"brush popping," 30
brushlands, 5, 66, 69
building materials, 46, 52–53, 85, 95; caliche blocks (*sillares*), 23, 26, 33–35, 39, 44, 45, 49, 92; *chipichil* (mortar), 26, 39, 45, 49; lumber, 39, 42; mesquite posts, 21, 24, 39; oil field pipe, 65, 72; stones, 16, 21; *vigas*, 26
Bureau of Animal Industries, 51
Bushland, R. C., 69
Bustamante's, 65

cactus, prickly pear, 52, 71, 83
Camargo (Mexico), 19, 20, 22, 30, 38, 39
Cameron County, 23, 53, 66
Canales, Gregorio, 37
Canary Islands, 9
Caribbean, 9
Carnestolendas. *See* Rancho Davis.
Casa Blanca grant, 39
Castillo, Acario, 98
cattle. *See* livestock.
cattle breeds, Angus, 69; Barrenda, 11; Brahman, 50, 69; Durham, 50;

ganado prieto, 11; Hereford, 50, 69; Retinto, 11; Santa Gertrudis, 50, 51, 69, 82; Shorthorn, 50; Texas Longhorn, 12, 50, 69
cattle drives, 9, 15, 29, 40–41, 51, 68
cemeteries, 22, 28, 89–90, 95
Cerralvo (Mexico), 19
chapels (*visitas*), 16, 21, 28, 95
Chapman, P. A., 67
Chapman Ranch, 67
Charles V, Emperor of Spain, 11
Chicago, Illinois, 40
Chicago Ranch. *See* Armstrong Ranch
Chihuahua (Mexico), 16, 21
Chiltipín Grant, 22
Chisholm Trail, 41
church. *See* religion
chutes, 70, 83, 96
Civil War (American), 15, 29, 40
Closs, Father Joseph Marie, 27–28
clothing, 21, 27; cowboy, 83; vaquero, 13, 28–29, 30, 42, 83
Coahuila (Mexico), 16, 19, 20, 23
Coastal Prairie, 4–5
College of Zacatecas, 7
Collins station, 51
Colombus, Christopher, 10, 11
Congrecación del Refugio. *See* Matamoros.
Corpus Christi, Texas, 37, 38, 39, 41, 42, 46, 49, 51, 52, 53, 64, 66, 67, 95
Corralitos, 20, 21, 22
corrals, 24, 36, 39, 42, 47, 52, 71, 83, 96
correr el gallo. See entertainment
Cortes, Hernán, 11
cow camp (*corrida*), 29–30, 53, 68
cowboys, 15, 41, 50, 51–52, 59, 67, 68, 70, 71, 76, 79, 83, 96, 99, 100
Cuervo, José Tienda de, 21
currency, 66

117